Elijah

Prophet of Power

BY THE SAME AUTHOR

Splendor from the Sea
As a Tree Grows
Bold under God—A Fond Look at a Frontier Preacher
A Shepherd Looks at Psalm 23
A Layman Looks at the Lord's Prayer
Rabboni—Which Is to Say, Master
A Shepherd Looks at the Good Shepherd and His Sheep
A Gardener Looks at the Fruits of the Spirit
Mighty Man of Valor—Gideon
Mountain Splendor
Taming Tension
Expendable
Still Waters
A Child Looks at Psalm 23
Ocean Glory
Walking with God
On Wilderness Trails
Elijah—Prophet of Power
Salt for Society
A Layman Looks at the Lamb of God
Lessons from a Sheep Dog
Wonder o' the Wind
Joshua—Man of Fearless Faith
A Layman Looks at the Love of God
Sea Edge
Chosen Vessels
David I
David II

W. Phillip Keller

WORD PUBLISHING
Dallas · London · Sydney · Singapore

To

the lay people

in

various countries

who

have learned much

from

Elijah's life

ISBN 0-8499-0266-5
ISBN 0-8449-3069-3 (paperback)
Library of Congress Catalog Card Number: 80-52162

Printed in the United States of America

898 RRD 9 8 7 6 5 4 3

Contents

In Appreciation

This is to thank the many lay people, who, after studying the life of Elijah with me, asked that the material be put into book form. This work is my response to their encouragement.

My wife Ursula, cheerful companion in the typing, has done a splendid piece of work in turning out an excellent manuscript.

Also I am grateful to Mr. Al Bryant, senior editor of Word Books, for recognizing the ministry this book might have among God's people.

There has been a special joy, a unique sense of delight in writing this biography of Elijah. May some of the enthusiasm granted to me by God's Gracious Spirit, be passed on to the reader.

A Word about This Book

For at least seven years a secret, special desire has burned within me to write a book on the life of Elijah. Along with Enoch, Joshua and Gideon, this "prophet of power" has been one of my four favorite Old Testament heroes.

His life has made an enormous impact upon my own understanding of how God deals with men. From Elijah's walk with God there have come clear lessons of great benefit to me, as well as others with whom these studies were shared.

My sincere hope is that readers will derive deep and helpful insights from the book that will widen the horizons of their spiritual understanding. May these pages not only be a pleasure to read, but provide godly incentives toward a closer walk with Christ.

What is more, I pray earnestly that this book will be used of God to quicken and energize some readers to become men and women of power in their generation. Perhaps you will be one of those people. Perhaps through these pages you will be called to special service for God just as Elijah was in his day.

1

The Temper of the Times

Only a little more than fifty years had elapsed in Israel's history since the new nation had stood at its pinnacle of power under David and Solomon. Less than one short century had seen the kingdom of God's special people retrogress from righteous rulership to the most rampant evil.

There had ascended to the throne of Israel a dreadful individual of whom it was said, "He did 'evil above all that were before' him" (1 Kings 14:9). No previous monarch had such a penchant for perverseness as had Ahab. He was literally addicted to evil. Wickedness was a way of life for him. He and his atrocious, fierce queen Jezebel wallowed in lewdness.

We can only begin to understand the character of God's chosen spokesman of this period, as we see it standing starkly against the darkness of his times. Elijah the desert nomad, the burning firebrand from the wilderness wastes east of Jordan, flames white hot, incandescent with indignation, against the evil blackness of his times.

In bold, blazing contrast lie the elements of goodness and evil; righteousness and wickedness. Debauchery and divinity are pitted against each other on the stage of Israel's horrendous history. Perhaps at no period in her whole agonizing story, since Moses faced Pharaoh, had there been such a convulsive confrontation.

As with the great prophet Moses, who spoke on behalf of God to the generation of his times, so again the Lord had sent a spokesman, a seer, to cry out against the decay of his day. Elijah was that burning, blazing, fearless firebrand who stands among the famous desert prophets called of God to challenge his people. Moses, Elijah, John the Baptist—they were unique to their time.

The goodness, the greatness, the godliness of this rough-hewn man can only be measured against the cankerous corruption of his culture. Religious, moral and social rot were consuming Israel like gangrene in an injured limb. The entire body and life of God's own chosen nation were decaying and dying under the influence of inner moral corruption.

Ahab the insolent, despicable monarch had blatantly repudiated and rejected the Lord Jehovah, God of Israel. Without a qualm he had plunged headlong into the appalling rituals and sexual orgies of Baal and Ashteroth. These were pagan deities dedicated to licentiousness, sexual perversion, violence and unbridled greed.

Again and again Israel had been warned that to pursue the gods and goddesses of Canaan would mean utter calamity. Over and over this chosen race of God's special people had been challenged to separate themselves from the corruption of false heathen cults. Time after time they had been told that to turn their backs on the Lord in pursuit of pagan practices was to invite total destruction.

But the warnings had been ignored. The temple prostitution of both men and women; the sexual licentiousness; the greed for gain; the rabid addiction to violence and revolt had found a ready response in the affections of both Ahab and Jezebel as well as their subject people.

Jezebel, of course, had been reared amid the pagan rituals of Baal. Her father was Ethbaal, king of the Zidonians and priest of Ashteroth, in whose domain the worship of Baal was perpetually practiced. She was simply doing what she had always done. But tragically for Israel her perversion was pressed upon both her husband, their king, and ultimately all the citizens.

The evil alliance between Ahab and Jezebel was more than merely a malevolent marriage. It was the subjection of an entire nation to the sinister influences that were determined to destroy her as the people of God.

It was a desperate hour of darkness for Israel.

Though perhaps oblivious to their danger, this people stood in mortal peril of total extinction. Their destruction would come, not from without, but from moral decay within.

And as is his habit in such situations, God found a man, a solitary soul, a fierce desert hawk, to send to his people in their peril. Elijah would come out of the dry dongas and wilderness wastes east of Jordan to challenge Ahab and call Israel to repentance. It would be her only remedy, her sole salvation from utter ruin and total degradation.

The parallels with our own period in history are starkly sobering. We in the Western world have had a godly heritage. The constitutions of our countries were grounded upon the declarations of God's Word. Our forefathers were those who revered and respected righteousness. Our system of jurisprudence, law and order was based upon the laws of God. As a free society we found our strength and fortitude in following the commands of Christ. We called ourselves a Christian people, who put their trust in God.

Much of that has changed. Israel has not been the

only nation, during its tragic history, to turn its back upon God. She has not been alone in rejecting and repudiating the righteousness required of her by a concerned and compassionate Jehovah. It was the Lord God who delivered Israel from her slavemasters in Egypt. It was he who led her through the desert wastes to the land of abundant promise in Palestine. It was he who established her there as a great and powerful people under Joshua. Yet she had spurned him. And in great seriousness may it be said here, we are doing the same in our day.

The temper of the time is to turn our backs on God. Everywhere there are those in positions of power and prominence who would have us repudiate righteousness and reject the laws of the Lord. Scorn and ridicule are heaped upon those who seek to serve God. The Christian is becoming an object of contempt.

Steadily, surely, insidiously we are a people given to preoccupation with sex and perversion of this great gift. We are becoming addicted to affluence and greed for gain. We revel in revolt and violence. For so-called "social success," we are selling ourselves short. Corruption and moral decay are destroying the foundations of our society grounded on a deep reverence for God and his laws.

Like ancient Israel in Ahab's day we are beginning to behave as if God really did not exist. He is totally ignored in most of our educational systems. He is regarded as irrelevant to our age of scientific technology. We are so completely preoccupied with our own sophisticated plans and programs, so caught up in our own petty pastimes and pursuits that the purposes of God for us are completely bypassed.

This was Ahab's position at the point when God's prophet of power stepped into his sordid career. Ahab had even planted a sacred grove of trees for the worship of Ashteroth, the goddess of sex and violence.

He was sure both he and Jezebel would be around a very long time to indulge themselves with the male and female prostitutes of this spot.

They assumed, rather naively, that they could do as they wished without any outside interference from the Lord. After all they had rejected his authority so they foolishly assumed that he would just go away or disappear if they simply chose to ignore his rule.

It so happens God doesn't do that. The laws he has ordained for us have only our own best interests in view. They are inexorable principles for proper and prosperous human conduct. Flaunt them and they will flatten you, not because God is vindictive or vengeful but simply because his eternal principles of appropriate human behavior are inviolate. One does not break God's laws. Rather his laws break those who transgress them. It is inevitable.

This Ahab and Jezebel were to learn to their sorrow and chagrin.

This Israel was to see and suffer.

One day, amid all the folly and fury of Israel's frivolity the prophet of God came and stood before Ahab. His name was *Elijah*. It meant "My God is Jehovah (the Lord)." This was in sharp and violent contrast to the god of Ahab, Baal, with his addiction to sex and affluence, or the goddess of Jezebel, Ashteroth, with her accent on violence and licentiousness.

Elijah's first powerful, penetrating announcement was, *"The Lord God of Israel liveth"* (1 Kings 17:1). He is not dead! He has not disappeared. He has not departed. God is very much alive—active, at work, here!

Elijah's second stabbing, searing statement was: *"It is before him that I stand and whom I serve"* (see 1 Kings 17:1).

It was enough to shatter the self-complacency of not only Ahab, but all his palace retinue, including the heartless and cunning Jezebel. Elijah had flung down the gauntlet of his challenge at the very nerve center of his country and people.

The desert prophet had been bold enough and brave enough to beard both the lion and the lioness in their lair. What if Ahab was king? What if Jezebel was queen? What if all Israel had gone a whoring after the prostitutes of Baal and Ashteroth? He, Elijah, servant of the most High God, would not be silent. He would no longer be still, left unheard, unnoticed in the blinding heat and desert dust of the trans-Jordan wastes.

He would raise his voice.

He would speak for his God.

He would sound the alarm that all was not well with Israel.

Proof of this would be a dreadful drought.

Year would follow year; season would succeed season; month would merge into month; day would die into day without a touch of dew or drop of rain to refresh the land. Under burning skies, searing sun and desert heat, grass, plants, trees, crops, birds, animals, adults and children would die of thirst and hunger.

It was a frightful forecast.

It was made without ostentation or fanfare.

It was a straightforward pronouncement of positive proof that God was alive, active in the affairs of men and nations.

And with that simple, direct statement Elijah left the presence of the king. He had delivered his message from the Lord. If his audience was skeptical as to his authenticity, subsequent events would soon prove his credentials were correct and granted by God.

The misdemeanor of Ahab and his nation had not passed unnoticed. In pride, arrogance and stubborn self-will Ahab had set out to do wrong. He little realized that in turn it is God who sets himself to resist the proud. It is he who humbles the arrogant. It is he who brings to dust the most elaborate designs and grandiose schemes of godless men.

In the latter half of the twentieth century there has been, in Christian circles, an overwhelming emphasis placed upon preaching about the *love* of God. And in its own way this has done great good. But at the same time there has been a pronounced tendency to set aside and pass over the righteousness and justice of God. The net result is that some people assume they can sin with impunity. They look lightly on lawlessness and lewdness.

But God does not. He never can. His impeccable character demands that justice be done, that sin be dealt with, that wrongdoing be counterbalanced.

This is a divine principle and it is well for us who live in our modern hedonistic society to see it. A day of divine reckoning is bound to come. Preoccupation with luxury, ease, sexual perversion, licentiousness and lawlessness will inevitably bring a counteraction of divine intervention.

What a man, a family or a nation plants and cultivates as its priority is bound to produce its own eventual crop of compensation, be it good or evil.

1 Kings 17:1–7

2

The Brook Cherith and the Ravens of God

The challenge which Elijah had flung in Ahab's face was not only a confrontation with his evil conduct, but also an outright attack on the power of Baal. This pagan god of the Canaanites was sometimes called "the storm god." He was the one who allegedly brought rain, showers, mist and dew to the parched land of Palestine. It was in his power to provide the abundance which guaranteed fertility of the fields, fertility of the flocks and fertility among his foolish followers.

Elijah's fearless assault was made in his own steadfast confidence in God. It was the Lord, Jehovah, who controlled climate. It was his God who, at his pleasure, could give or withhold beneficial weather. All good gifts and all perfects gifts including rain, mist, dew and sunshine came down from God (see James 1:17, Matt. 5:45).

Elijah challenged the power of Baal to produce any rain at any time anywhere. There would be devastating drought as proof positive that this pagan deity was a sham created by the fantasy of man.

But because of the temper of the times any man who took such a daring stand of faith in God was marked for liquidation. Jezebel was a violent woman. She adored a violent goddess, Ashteroth. She would not hesitate an instant to use violence to wipe out any antagonist. Elijah was no exception. He immediately was considered to be public enemy number one. He must pay, and pay with his very life, for daring to flaunt her fury.

The net result of their violent confrontation was for God to direct Elijah to go underground. No longer would he be the blazing desert firebrand flinging fiery tirades at Ahab and Jezebel, Baal and Ashteroth. He would vanish from view. He would drop out of sight, submerged in the desert wastes.

The command to do this came from God. It was not Elijah's idea. With his powerful, vehement personality Elijah would much have preferred to remain in the public eye. Undoubtedly his own convictions were that the battle between good and evil, God and Baal, would have gone much better in full view of Israel where the fierce impact of his fearless faith in God would be fully exposed for all to see.

But God's ways and man's ways are often diametrically different—even positively opposed. God does not always resort to the spectacular, dramatic methods which mean so much to men. Sometimes his greatest conquests are accomplished with the least apparent processes.

At this point in Elijah's career being sent into the desolate obscurity of a desert donga where a filthy little flow of polluted water cut its way through the dry, barren, treeless hills was a fierce test of his faith in God. The brook Cherith was no babbling, singing mountain stream as so many preachers and painters have portrayed it. Its very name means "the cutting place" where a small seep of water had worn away the rock and stone to form a deep defile in the desert.

Going to Cherith for Elijah was equivalent to going into oblivion. It was going into obscurity. It was going into darkness, degradation and desolation. It is a mark of the stature of the man that he went at all, showing how sensitive he was to the voice of God's Spirit.

Most of us dread the dark defiles in life. We don't want to be in the valleys, and we shun the shadows. We aren't at all interested in the "cutting" experiences. We much prefer to be in the limelight of center stage where all the action is. We love to display our derring-do in the thrust and parry of dramatic events. Any of us can be heroic in the heat of heady battles.

It takes a much greater caliber of character to go down into the cutting canyons of Cherith alone with God.

For us, as for Elijah, there has to be a Cherith before there can be a Carmel. There has to be a cross before there can be a crown. There has to be death to self-aggrandizement before there can spring up an irresistible new life of power with God.

The interlude at Cherith was much more than one of simple isolation, obscurity or oblivion. It was infinitely more for Elijah than merely being "set aside on the shelf"—repugnant as that may have seemed for such a man of action.

It was also an incredible humiliation. Only as we see the implications of his time in the context of ancient Hebrew culture will we comprehend Elijah's cutting, awesome, excruciating agony.

God's word to him was that he would be fed there by wild ravens. It all sounds so poetic. In truth for Elijah this was appalling.

Ravens are ubiquitous birds, found the world over on every continent. All through human history both in the Orient and the Occident they have been regarded as an omen of misfortune, tragedy, death. In the Hebrew tradition they were regarded as unclean, contaminated and an abomination because of their scavenging habits.

Ravens normally were carrion eaters. They consumed the scraps of offal and putrifying flesh that remained on carcasses left by the jackals and hyenas of the desert. Any discarded fragments of bad food or rotten wastes that were flung outside the village walls were pounced upon by ravens. Their coarse cries were a common sound in the desert wastes. They were bold, black birds surviving on scraps of hide, bits of bone and remnants of rubbish.

It was on such frightful fare that Elijah would have to survive at Cherith. The ravens of God did not bring him sirloin steak and fresh baked bread. They brought him garbage.

This all sounds repulsive and abhorrent to us. The more so if we have been led to believe naïvely and falsely that life for God's person must be always beautiful and comfortable and cozy. It simply is not so.

Christ's own words to his followers were: *"In the world ye shall have tribulation; but be of good cheer; I have overcome the world"* (John 16:33). The psalmist of old reiterated the same truth: *"Many are the afflictions of the righteous; but the Lord delivereth him out of them all"* (Ps. 34:19). Read also Hebrews 11:36–40.

It can cost a great deal to follow Christ.

It can be a cutting ordeal to do God's will.

It can humiliate us. It can test and refine our faith in him.

For Elijah, the interval at Cherith was one of enormous implications. If he could stand the solitude, the isolation, the immobilization, the defamation, and the humiliation, then he could endure almost anything.

It is worthy of note, too, that in no way was he exempt from the trauma of his times. The desperate drought that descended to desiccate and destroy the countryside had just as great an impact upon him as anyone else. Even the little trickle of water that he must share with the wild ravens, desert animals and local livestock began to dry up. Its waters may well have been muddied and murky from the trampling of hooves and the debris of birds and reptiles. It may also have been polluted by the accumulation of scum and algae that proliferate during hot, dry weather.

No, his daily drink from this contaminated little water course of slimy, soupy, awful water was not the sort of thing any man would relish—not even a rough desert nomad like Elijah who knew fully what it was to survive in the savage, stern and cruel environment of the trans-Jordan. His home territory of Gilead was famous for its fierce heat. Here daytime temperatures often exceeded 120° by midafternoon. Even in the sparse shade of some scrawny desert bush or barren, overhanging rock a man could die.

In spite of all this: In spite of the dreadful diet: In spite of the diabolical drink: In spite of the desert drought Elijah stuck it out at Cherith.

It was the place of God's appointment for him at that point in time. It was the arrangement made for his survival. It was the fierce furnace of affliction that would refine his faith in God. He did not try to duck out of it.

It was God who had sent him to Cherith.

It was God who supported him in Cherith.

It was God who would take him out of Cherith.

This was God's best will for his life. To us and to others looking on it may have seemed a wasted interval. In our ignorance we stand back appalled and horrified. Beneath our breaths we protest, "Surely he didn't have to go through all this—there must have been a better way."

No, God's ways and our ways are not the same. His methods and ours are not the same. His methods for turning out tough, triumphant people and ours are not the same.

It was Peter who protested to Christ that he should not go up to Jerusalem to be tormented and tortured by the crass cruelty of his contemporaries. Our Lord's reply to the big fisherman was, *"You stand right in my path, Peter, when you look at things from man's point of view and not from God's"* (Matt. 16:23, Phillips).

Happily for Elijah he made no attempt either to escape from or sidestep his call to Cherith. He was willing to go wherever God sent him. He was willing to remain in the most repulsive situation as long as it was the place of God's special arrangement for him. He was willing to drink to the dregs the cup of suffering and humiliation appointed for him. As with our Lord, so with him, his conduct speaks in powerful accents to all of us—*"Not my will but thine be done!"*

This is faith in action. This is confidence in God. This is to declare unhesitatingly, "Oh God, no matter how awful my circumstances, you do know best. Do what you will—all is well! It is for my ultimate good! For the shaping of my character to yours!"

3

Elijah Goes to Zarephath

Elijah's interlude at Cherith was not altogether just a dark or difficult interval in his life. It had its benefits. There were compensations amid his loneliness. God had not forsaken him in that desolate spot. He never does!

It was probably true that the only audible sounds he heard were the ravenous cries of the ravens who came winging in over him to drop their fragments of flesh and food. In the distance there would be the haunting howl of the hyenas or yap of jackals at the carcass of an animal that had died in the drought. No doubt the dry, desperate desert winds moaned around the rugged, hot rocks of his canyon hideout.

But the wind of God's Spirit also stirred in that solitary spot. There the Lord communed with Elijah in the depths of his spirit. For if nothing else this fierce desert prophet was alert and keenly sensitive to the voice of his God. He knew with an acute inner intuition the impulses which came to him from God.

The brook Cherith was more than a "cutting place" for Elijah, it was also a "communion place." Here by the shrinking trickle of murky water, amid the intense silence of the desert he came into intimate contact with his God.

It is in our dark hours, amid those lonely moments when we seem so all alone, that most often we discover the intense nearness of Christ. He is here. He does reveal himself. He does commune with us. He does speak. He does direct—if we are receptive and attuned to his intentions.

Elijah was! It must be said to his eternal credit that the secret to the power of this flaming prophet was his instant and ready obedience to the voice of God. What the Lord said, he did!

And the next command which came was even more drastic than the first which sent him to Cherith. Now he was to travel north and west across the full breadth of this sun-bleached land. His next stopping spot would be Zarephath, a small village on the outskirts of Zidon, a seaside town on the Mediterranean coast.

The Sidonians were foreigners to the people of Israel. They were a seafaring race descended from the ancient and fierce Phoenicians who for centuries dominated the seaways of this inland ocean. For Elijah to go to Zarephath was to go into enemy territory! At least at Cherith he had been back on his old desert terrain familiar to him from boyhood.

But going to Zarephath was to be sent into a strange and hostile setting. Hostile because always, ever, from their earliest times, the people of Zidon had worshiped Baal. In fact, this was the citadel of Ethbaal, king of the Zidonians whose daughter Jezebel had corrupted Ahab.

God was asking Elijah to suddenly step out of the safe obscurity of a desert canyon straight onto the doorstep of his implacable enemy Baal. There Elijah was to live in full view of his most violent opponents, within arrow shot of the central stronghold of the heathen god he hated.

A lesser man would have blanched at such orders. He would have protested vehemently at such a risky mission. He might well have buckled under such pressure.

But not Elijah. The word of the Lord to him was "Arise, get thee to Zarephath . . . and dwell there" (1 Kings 17:9). So he did just that. It all sounds so simple, so straightforward. In truth it was much tougher than ever going to Cherith. For at Zarephath Elijah was to be tested and toughened in a deep moral and spiritual dimension.

Zarephath means "the place of refining." And it would be just that for Elijah. At Cherith God had begun his rough chiselling on this rugged character. At Zarephath there would be further polishing and finishing to fit him for the formidable future.

The fact that he had been assured that a widow there would provide for him was really little consolation. After all, the ancient traditions relating to widows and orphans were severe and strictly observed. One did not impose upon a widow and her offspring. One did not in any way take unfair advantage of these unfortunate members of society. To do so was to incur the wrath of God and the stigma of society.

No, indeed, a wandering mendicant, even if he was the servant of God and spoke for the Lord, had no legitimate license to seek support or succor from a widow. To do so was to fly in the face of convention.

Here, for example, is but one clear injunction on this very delicate matter: *"Ye shall not afflict any widow, or fatherless child. If thou afflict them in any wise, and they cry at all unto me, I will surely hear their cry; and my wrath shall wax hot, and I will kill you with the sword; and your wives shall be widows, and your children fatherless"* (Exod. 22:22–24).

Elijah knew all about this. He was not naïve. Nor was he oblivious to the enormous implications of his call to go and share the meager Spartan fare of a widow woman whose life and that of her son teetered on the brink of extinction because of the terrible drought that decimated the countryside.

No indeed. He had to be sure, very sure indeed, that his summons to Zarephath came clearly, unmistakably from God and not just from his own subconscious mind.

There was double danger for Elijah in this assignment. It is not obvious to us perhaps, but for him it was really a traumatic test. Again it must be understood in the context of the culture of his times.

The people of Israel were given very clear instructions on exactly how widows and orphans were to be supported in their agrarian society. Fields and crops were not to be harvested utterly clean. The gleanings were to be the portion for the impoverished.

The grapevines were to be picked over only once. The ripe clusters which were missed and remained hidden by leaves were the legitimate leavings for widows and orphans to gather up in glee. The olive trees were to be beaten only one time. Any fruit that did not fall then was to remain as a supply for the widows and fatherless who followed behind the beaters to collect their portion (see Deut. 24:19–21).

All of this was fine. It was a beautiful and generous arrangement made by God for widows and orphans.

But at the word of Elijah, the skies had turned to burning brass; the clouds of rain had blown away into desert dust; the soil had set hard as concrete under the searing sun and there were no crops, no grain, no grapes, no olives for anyone anywhere, let alone widows and orphans.

Elijah was acutely aware and painfully self-conscious of his rôle as centerpiece in this whole dreadful drama of the drought that now paralyzed Palestine. One could legitimately lay the blame for the terrible famine at his feet. He knew this. He knew he was regarded as the one who troubled Israel—yes, troubled the whole country including neighboring Sidon.

Did he have any right, really, to go and reside with a widow woman whose lot in life had become unbearable because of the drought and famine? It was a soul-searching question! It was an issue that made a man examine his motives and actions with intense earnestness.

He had to be absolutely sure that what he was doing was God directed. It is too easy to move through life making decisions based upon our own selfish, self-centered inclinations. As God's people we must examine our priorities, we must establish clearly that our commands do indeed come from Christ and not from just the accidental circumstances around us.

Elijah was sure he was in harmony with God's will for him. Without questioning further he came to Zidon. There he soon found the desperate, destitute widow outside the village gates of Zarephath searching for a few scraps of wood and twigs of brush for her fire.

She was apparently too poor to procure fuel for herself from the dealers in town. So, in shame and humility she had gone into the country to collect what sticks she could to fuel the last fire she thought she would ever need to make. It was the end for her and her son. Elijah's drought had done its deadly deed. The famine had finished off her family. This was the termination of the torturous path she had trod in life.

Elijah—brown, burned with desert sun, bearded with months of hairy growth, wrapped in a dusty mantle—came up to her boldly, begging for a drink of water. His dried, parched, cracked lips and swollen tongue had not tasted good clean, clear water for a long, long time.

To ask such a favor of a strange woman was an act of tremendous humiliation. It was bad enough to come here seeking shelter from a widow. It was the ultimate degradation to take any food or drink from her fingers. A man in that culture simply did not condescend, normally, to partake of that which a woman's hands had handled.

All of this went against his grain. His whole demeanor was contrary to convention. Elijah, the proud, powerful, passionate prophet from the desert, was simply doing what God had asked. It was like death to Elijah. It would be life to the widow and her orphan son.

The fact was Elijah needed the widow to accomplish the Lord's refining work in his character. And the widow desperately needed Elijah to once more feel wanted, needed, useful. Elijah could have acted arrogantly and independently. He could have been proud and self-sufficient. In so doing he would have impoverished both himself and the woman to whom God sent him.

Too many of us in our sophisticated twentieth-century society try "to go it alone." We are reluctant to reveal our needs to others. We refuse to let others reach out to help or support us. In our proud, self-assured independence we are poorer than we think. Some of the closest, dearest, most precious bonds of friendship are forged when we pocket our pride and ask someone to assist us. We enrich them in so doing.

4

A Handful of Flour and a Drop of Oil

The widow's contact with the formidable prophet of power had an electrifying impact upon her. She promptly left her search for sticks and kindling to fetch him a drink of water. Her immediate attention had been shifted from herself and her suffering to that of another. Her focus had been reoriented and redirected toward someone else in distress.

This is one of the special secrets to strength and serenity in human relationships. There is always someone else near at hand whose affliction and burdens are greater than our own. The instant we step out to help lift their load even a little, our own becomes lighter and less onerous to bear. We actually gain strength and sense new serenity sweep into our souls as we share ourselves with others.

As the widow went for water, precious, precious fluid with which to refresh the desert man, Elijah called to her, asking that she also bring him a bite of bread. A bit of home-made bread would be such a treat after living on scraps brought by the ravens for so many months.

The widow stopped short in her tracks. She didn't mind fetching water that came from the village well. But to bring bread from the meager remnant that remained at the bottom of her empty flour bin was asking a bit too much. Apparently she felt that she was really being put upon, for she protested in despair that to bring Elijah a freshly baked fragment of food was to exhaust all her resources. It spelled out sure starvation for both herself and her son.

"I only have a tiny woman's handful of flour left in my container! There is but a drop of oil with which to prepare it left in my jar! It is only barely enough for a last mouthful for me and my son."

Subconsciously she was saying to herself, and to Elijah, and to God, whom she apparently did not know personally: "You have no right to afflict the widow and the fatherless! You are taking unfair advantage of us! You are transgressing the law of God."

It was a frightening moment for her. It was also a frightening moment for Elijah. Both of them were at an impasse. What would come of it? Would she and her son perish from starvation? Would the desert prophet be destroyed for his overbearing imposition upon this poor woman? Was he being unfair and unjust to ask so much?

Life is often like that for all of us. Those in need do make demands upon us. It seems sometimes that we can do little to alleviate their anguish. Like the woman we can run to the well of our community resources to find refreshment for them. Perhaps we can turn to the church or pastor or some other social agency from whom we all derive help to meet the need. We may even be bold enough to run to Christ, the very fountain of living water, to find refreshment for the thirsting ones who come to us in their despair.

But if their plight is pressed upon us even more personally to the point that they want a share of our bread and butter, we begin to protest. We claim our resources are limited. We insist that there is simply not enough for both us and them. We are sure that someone will be forced to the wall . . . and that it is asking us far too much.

Few of us ever seem to discover that true sacrifice for another comes out of our very survival, never out of our surplus. We know nothing about genuine self-giving and self-sharing until our own self-survival is literally put on the line. Such a thought terrifies most of us!

And it was exactly here that the widow stood when Elijah said to her: "Lady, just carry on and bake the very last *japati* [a pancake-like piece of peasant bread] for yourself and your son. *But first make me one from the handful of flour and drop of oil that remains!*"

It must be said to Elijah's great credit that he did not allow the woman's panic and fear to be transmitted to himself. It is a measure of the man's unshakable confidence in God that he continued to press his point upon her. He knew full well that he could never depend upon her meager resources to support both him and her. Their mutual support and sustenance both for the moment and for as long as the famine lasted would have to come from the Lord. His faith was grounded, not in a handful of flour and a drop of oil, but in the faithfulness of God.

Too many of us as Christians take our cue in life from our contemporaries. We allow the world's view of life—its proneness to panic, its fear of the future, its limited resources—to condition both our outlook and behavior. Like the widow woman we cry out that there is simply not enough to share or spare. We contend that our resources are reaching the point of exhaustion. We focus in on the possibility of failure. We see only the severe limitations of what there is at hand.

Elijah did not succumb to this sort of mindset! He refused to let the widow's woeful outlook cloud or obscure his view of what God could do. His unshakable and sure conviction was that God had sent him to Zarephath. God had sent him to reside with this destitute widow. God would send him and her and her family all that was needed to survive the dreadful drought.

God does not indulge in embarrassing those who put their confidence in him. He honors those who honor him. He vindicates the faith of any man or woman who invests their trust in his capacity to meet his commitments to them. He is pleased to find those who recognize His sterling character.

It is to such people that Christ comes and fills their lives to overflowing, not only with spiritual benefits, but also with moral and material resources beyond their fondest dreams.

The powerful prophet looked calmly and quietly at the distraught widow. His words were a soothing, healing ointment to her tempestuous fears. *"Don't be afraid. Don't worry. Don't panic. The Lord can and will supply all the flour and oil we shall ever require."*

This was faith in action.

This was Elijah's powerful, positive response to the word spoken by God.

It demonstrated that he had an unshakable confidence in the character of Jehovah, God. He would come through. He would supply flour and oil, bread and butter, for all of them throughout the famine.

This was to exercise faith not only for himself, but also on behalf of others. His God was alive! His God was active! His God would deliver them out of their dilemma!

This was faith without fear.

It was straightforward obedience to the declared will and wishes of the Lord. It was the secret of Elijah's success, the key to the prophet's power.

The widow may not have had this intimate acquaintance with God, but Elijah did. And the contagion of his calm confidence in the utter reliability of God caught up the woman in her despair and moved her, too, to act in faith.

"Just bake me some bread first, and you will see that God will supply sufficient for all the rest."

It was a challenge from which, happily, the desperate woman did not recoil. Instead she set out to do what she had been asked to do. She went to fetch the drink of water for the prophet. She went to prepare, not the last, but the first of hundreds of meals from her handful of flour and mere drop of oil.

The principle at work here is one ordained of God for the benefit of his people. Yet it is one scoffed at and scorned by a cynical, skeptical humanistic society.

That principle is the one so clearly stated over and over in God's Word but perhaps best phrased by our Lord when he said: *"Seek ye first the kingdom of God, and his righteousness; and all these things shall be added unto you"* (Matt. 6:33).

It is the one prepared to unhesitatingly give to God whatever is in his possession who finds it multiplied over and over. It was the little lad who placed his rolls and sardines in Jesus' strong hands, instead of in his own stomach, who saw them increased to feed thousands of others around him who were also hungry.

It was the widow's willingness to take her last handful of flour and final tiny drop of oil to bake a *japati* for Elijah who saw her supplies stretched out to feed a whole family through months and months of famine. It is not what we possess that matters, but it is how we hold it in our hands. Do we timidly, hesitatingly clutch our little store close to our chests? Are we afraid it will not be enough? Are we concerned our resources will run out?

Try God and find out!

Put him first. Open wide the tightly clutching

fingers. Hold lightly in an open hand whatever you have. Give it away gladly, gleefully to God and to his people. As it is shared with others it is shared with him (read Matt. 25:14–46).

The results will be astounding.

The resources will be replenished again and again.

The meager handful and tiny drop will be multiplied to minister to a hundred others.

The widow gave her fragments of food. God took them to feed all of her family as well as Elijah throughout the famine. Little is much when God is in it.

Anything turned over to God can be touched and transformed to take care of thousands around us. He waits only for our response.

5

Death of the Widow's Son

As so frequently happens in life, the happy situation in the widow's humble home, supplied as it was with enough to eat, did not last long. A shadow fell across the doorstep one day, the gaunt gray shadow of disease and death. Her son was taken ill, and gradually his condition grew worse until at last he succumbed.

It was a traumatic event for the little lad's mother. She had been sure when Elijah first appeared on the scene that both she and her son would perish from starvation. Then the powerful prophet had produced a dramatic turnaround in their affairs. Now she had been equally sure all of them would survive as day after day flour and oil were dramatically supplied to sustain them.

So the boy's death was a double blow. Hope raised then suddenly shattered is excruciatingly painful. It drains away the confidence and fortitude of those whose hearts have been crushed. It crumbles one's will to live. It destroys the very joy of living.

For the widow her son's terminal illness was taken as a direct and personal punishment from God. She was sure that somehow this was divine judgment for her own past misdeeds. In short she was sure she had been "found out" by the fiery desert prophet who had come to her door begging for a handout of bread and water.

Why, oh why, had she ever allowed herself to become involved with him? Why had she ever permitted him to intrude into her affairs? What a fool she had been to give him room and shelter in the famine!

She was sure that she had made a false move in having anything to do with this man. Though her intentions toward Elijah had been good and pure, somehow things had gone wrong. It was worse now than if he had never come into her home. She had been double-crossed. And she was furious!

The whole scene is repeated ten thousand times in the lives of men and women who come in contact with the living Lord. People, somehow, are given to believe, either through wrong teaching or false preaching, that if they put their confidence in Christ; if they are obedient to his commands; if they act in forthright faith, all will be well for the rest of their days. They conclude somehow that they will automatically be exempted from the tragedy and turmoil of their times.

But this is simply not so. In the very nature of things, all of us, Christian and non-Christian alike, are caught up in the warp and woof of life's sorrow and suffering. All of us together are subject to pain. It is part and parcel of life's pattern. There are no exceptions. If it is not of a physical bodily dimension, then it may be mental, emotional, moral or spiritual.

The reason for this is simply that we live in a world where sin, evil, selfishness and Satan himself move and work in opposition to the good will of God. The counteraction of these formidable forces produces tensions, turmoil, trauma and suffering of a thousand sorts.

Yet amid all this, one great cardinal difference remains to distinguish between the Christian and non-

Christian—between the pagan and the believer. That difference lies in the way in which each faces the pain.

In this pagan woman's home we see the drama acted out in real life between her and Elijah, the man of God.

The woman reacted to the anguish that fell upon her with anger, hostility and bitterness. Holding her little son to her heaving bosom she lashed out at Elijah in wrath. Through her tears she told him bluntly it simply had to be his fault. After all, he was the one nearest at hand, so he was made her "whipping boy."

Sure, she may have made some wrong moves in life. She may have strayed at times from the straight and narrow way. But so what? Didn't everyone else? That was no reason for him to come meddling in her affairs. It would have been better if he had never shown up. So in her fury she soon forgot his benefits.

It is easy to do this. When suffering or sorrow suddenly engulfs us like a flood, we often quickly forget the goodness of our friends, our family, even our God. In self-pity and hurt we lash out against whoever is near at hand. We heap abuse upon husband or wife, parent or child, friend or neighbor. It must be someone's fault. There must be a scapegoat. It is all so unfair, so unjust, and in the tirade innocent bystanders bear the brunt of our abuse.

Elijah was in this invidious position. But it is beautiful to observe the magnificent behavior of this powerful prophet in the face of the woman's fury and frustration. Not for an instant did he allow his own emotions to counteract her false accusations. Not for a moment did he return railing for railing. Nor did he succumb to any desire for self-justification as most of us would have done.

What Elijah did was one of the most magnanimous gestures ever exhibited by a man of God.

In greatness, generosity and gentleness he reached

out his arms to the woman and took the dead body into his own embrace. They were in this suffering together; he and she. Her burden was also his burden. Her heartbreak was his heartbreak. Her pain was his pain.

He took the lifeless form of the little lad from her hot breast to his own bedroom. He lifted the load from her heart to his heart.

Not only was this exceedingly generous, but it was likewise exceedingly brave, for it was considered in the culture of those times a most heinous sin for a man of God even to touch a corpse. One simply had nothing to do with the dead belonging to strangers. It was different for one's own immediate kin. But the law of Moses forbade any priest from defiling himself with the dead (see Lev. 21:1–4).

What Elijah was saying to the widow woman by his bold action in taking her boy was this: "I have completely accepted you. I have taken you to my heart as my family. I love you as dearly as my own. We are one!"

This was total and complete identification of himself with the woman in her grief. It was bearing the burden of another. It was the identical action Christ took when he came among us to bear our burdens.

Everything in Elijah may well have recoiled from such a step. All of his traditions and teaching may have surfaced to prevent him from such humiliation. His inhibitions and self-conscious revulsion against such a gruesome, close encounter with the dead might have made him pause and hold back. But he was not that sort of person.

He was in the midst of pain, and he would taste it too. He would enter fully into the pathos of this hour. He would not shelter or shield himself from the suffering that surrounded him. He, too, would drink it to the dregs. Even if the woman by her vituperation had revealed that she had never really "accepted" him, Elijah was to show that he had fully accepted her.

His words to her were short, simple, stabbing. "Give me your son!" Let me absorb your hurt. Let me have your pain. Let me bear your burden. Let me take your troubles.

What condescension! What generosity! What a gracious gesture!

Quietly, calmly, Elijah carried the lad up to the loft of this humble home and laid him on his own sleeping pallet. There in that tiny room was to be a trysting place with God. It was God who gave; it was God who took away; blessed be his name.

It is significant Elijah did not attempt to perform any public miracle either before the widow or other members of her family who may have gathered around to mourn for the dead. He was a man alone with his Lord, beseeching God on behalf of another. There was not even a second guessing what God's motives may have been. All Elijah wanted was life from death.

Elijah did not believe that God had permitted the widow's son to perish as some punishment for her past. Instead he implicitly believed that the calamity had been allowed to come to this home to demonstrate the sublime sovereignty of Jehovah God. It was he alone who could revive, restore and rehabilitate the whole home.

God (his God, whom he served, and before whom he lived out his life with this pagan widow on the doorstep of Baal's stronghold) could not only give flour and oil in the midst of famine, but could bring life from death on behalf of the one who fully trusted him. Elijah wanted to see the woman not only gladly accept the benefits bestowed by God, but also to accept God himself. This obviously she had never done, just as she had never fully accepted Elijah.

The powerful prophet would not let anything deter

him from seeing that God's will was done in the widow's life and home. Without fuss or fanfare he stretched himself fully upon the prostrate corpse lying prone on his pallet. It was a gruesome thing to have to do. Fully, freely, fearlessly the determined desert firebrand extended himself upon the boy's body. His head to his head; his arms to his arms; his limbs to his limbs. This was total and complete identification with the dead. This was to drink fully and freely and fearlessly of death to his own self.

Only out of such utter selflessness; only out of such self-sacrifice; only out of such self-denial in sorrow and suffering for another could there come the infinite, irresistible, invincible life of God.

"Oh God," he moaned, "let this lad's life, your very life, life from above, come into this body again!"

Elijah was interceding with God for a revival. Bound that there should be renewal, he would not be denied. He was prepared to extend himself to the utmost to see it happen. He considered himself totally expendable in order to move the hand and heart of God. It did not matter what the personal cost, he was prepared to pay the price of consummate sacrifice to prevail with God.

1 Kings 17:22–24

6

The Lad Lives Again

The Lord God heard and heeded Elijah's heart cry.

It was a profound prayer arising from the innermost spirit of a man right with God and right with others. There was no cloud of wrongdoing obscuring this rugged prophet's view of his God. He saw him with a clear, unclouded conscience. His spiritual sight of Jehovah was not obscured or impaired by a darkened conscience the way the woman's had been (see James 5).

This is what is meant by the prayer of a righteous man. It is the powerful, profound longing of a spirit and soul in harmony with the will and wishes of God. It is a man's spirit moved upon by God's Spirit to express itself in groanings which cannot always be fully articulated in human syllables.

And as Elijah stretched himself upon the corpse there rose from his whole person an irresistible petition that God would bring life back into the boy's body. Such a prayer prevails with God. These are the prayers of intercession which have their origin with Christ himself, the author of our faith. They are transmitted to our spirits by his own gracious Spirit, who in turn helps us to lift them again to God for his approval. For in the end he, too, is the finisher and accomplisher of our faith: the One who sees our desires honored and vindicated, both for his own dear name's sake as well as our own benefit.

At this point, the mother of the boy was quite incapable of such a prayer. Her conscience was darkened by past wrongdoing in her life that had never been made right with God. Because of this her view of God was impaired. She was incapable of seeing him in his mercy and compassion. She sensed only, in some obscure way, that he had sent severe judgment on her and her son because of past sins. No wonder she abused Elijah as she did! Little marvel she could not pray for help in her hour of anguish.

It is the person with a cleansed conscience and an unclouded view of God, who comes to him boldly and unafraid, asking for great favors (Heb. 10:10–22).

God's response to Elijah was positive and prompt. The lad's life was restored. He did come alive again; he was revived.

It is noteworthy that the powerful prophet did not exploit the incident to try and prove his prowess with God. He did not make a great public display of the miraculous restoration. Instead, he quietly gathered the boy up into his strong arms and carried him back downstairs to the weeping widow.

Legend and tradition claim that this lad was later to become Elijah's servant. Scripture does not state this. Still it is a happy thought.

It is significant that at no point did the prophet ask or expect the widow to join him in praying for her child's recovery. Not once did he even hint that it would help if she too petitioned God.

God does not succumb to popular pressure or large scale lobbying. He is not prevailed upon either by sheer weight of numbers or the proliferation of numerous prayers. Some churches and some people have the strange concept that the more people who can be induced to pray at one time the greater will be the impact made upon God. Not so. Our Lord, speaking on the matter of prayer, made it abundantly clear that we are not heard either for the abundance of our prayers nor for their duration (read Matt. 6:1–15).

Rather, a person's prayers are respected and responded to on the basis of that individual's right relationship to God—on his clear, unclouded view of Christ and his ability to act on our behalf.

Elijah had gone into his little loft bedroom alone with a dead body in his arms. He came out of that closeted room with a restored child in his embrace. He saw his God and spoke to him. He believed God could deliver the lad. He saw it done. All simply because he was right with his Lord.

When Elijah first met the widow outside the village gates, gathering a handful of sticks for her last fire, she was sure she and her son had reached the end of the road. It took the touch of Elijah's life and the intervention of Elijah's God to show her that she was mistaken.

When Elijah took the limp, cold corpse of her son from her sobbing bosom and bore him up to his own bedroom, she was again sure this was the end. Once more it was the man of God whose presence and power proved her wrong. As Elijah placed the restored boy in her arms he remarked quietly, calmly, "See, your son is alive!"

The world view of life is one of despair. The Christian's view should be one of delight.

Contemporary society is jaded and jaundiced. The Christian community should be radiant and joyous.

The world smirks with casual, callous skepticism. The Christian must be buoyant with hope and confidence in God.

We both live on the same planet faced with the same

pain, perplexities, and problems. Yet our views are totally different, totally distinct, totally divergent from one another.

As someone has put it: "One man looks out the window and sees only mud after the rain. The other looks out and sees the stars after the storm."

The widow's response to her son's restoration is one of the most moving, most eloquent tributes ever paid by one human being to another.

As she pressed her boy's warm cheek to her own tear-stained face she declared emphatically—"*Elijah, now I know you are a man of God, and that what you say is truth*" (see 1 Kings 17:24).

God, very God, alive, alert, active, at work in this man by his own presence and Spirit, had not only made the boy alive, but he had brought her alive, too, to the living Lord. At last she had accepted not only Elijah, but even more important, Elijah's God.

What to her had seemed to be a dead-end road, God had seen fit to turn into a highway of holiness in walking with him.

1 Kings 18:1, 2

7

Elijah Complies with God's Command

Elijah spent a long time with the widow woman after her son was restored to life. The exact length of the powerful prophet's long wait for God's next word to him is not known precisely. But we gather from the reports of both the Old and New Testaments that it must have been close to three years, if not a little more.

James, in his Epistle, declared that the devastating drought lasted three years and six months. And if we assume that Elijah had camped at the brook Cherith for roughly six months or less until it dried up, then obviously his residence in the foreign village of Zarephath must have spanned some thirty-six months.

This is not a long time if one is at home, with one's own family and friends. But to be on foreign soil in residence with strangers for that period is a trying test. The more so when during the extended drought no word at all came from the Lord as to what his next move should be. No doubt rumors and reports had reached Elijah through the usual underground grapevine of human gossip that his life was being sought by the vicious and vindictive Jezebel.

She had been able to prevail on her weak-spined husband, Ahab, to have the prophets of God in Israel put to death. But out of them all Elijah, the most prized prey, had eluded her cruel grasp. Spies had been sent out all over Palestine, like hounds on a bloody trail, to try and find the desert firebrand. All of them had failed. Possibly because it had never entered anyone's mind that Elijah would be so daring and bold as to ensconce himself on the very doorstep of Jezebel's own home city.

Elijah's three long years of waiting to hear from God again were not only precarious but painfully slow in passing. He was a man of action, a spokesman for his Lord God Jehovah. To be incarcerated with the widow in a three-year stretch of silence was no easy thing.

This is true for most of us. We are an impatient people. We want action, instant action from God. We are reluctant to be sidelined. We often presume very wrongly that because we are not in the thick of things, somehow life is passing us by and we are losing out. We of the West are especially a people "on the go." We are tightly locked into a time-space concept and culture, convinced that our days must be consumed in feverish activity and a series of hectic dramatic events.

Most of us have never learned the secret of being "still" before God. We have never come to the maturity that accepts the quiet interludes in life as his provision for our welfare. We have not yet come to see that godly growth and godly attainment can proceed as rapidly in the quiet times and gentle retreats as they can in the heat and fury of action.

It takes some of us almost a lifetime to discover that our God is seldom if ever in a great rush or hurried frenzy as we humans are. In his infinite wisdom, care and love he takes great pains and long periods of time over his own sublime work, whether it be growing a great oak in the woods, or growing a great character in a person's career.

Often, as with Elijah, our Father will put us into the quiet place because he knows that is best for us. He alone knows what lies ahead. He knew the tremendous conflicts and flaming encounters that Elijah would soon have on Carmel. In such knowledge he also knew it was proper and appropriate that the powerful prophet be fully rested and refreshed for the battles ahead.

If our Lord invites us to come apart and be alone, still, quiet in the solitary place for a spell, let us be glad. We will be wise to accept these gentle interludes with grace. They are his fitting ground for great things ahead.

I recall vividly such a period of quiet waiting in my own life. I was far from my homeland on foreign soil. It seemed there was no word from God as to my next move in life.

Opportunities for service were nil. No matter where I turned every step seemed blocked to any advance. In anguish and agony of spirit I would stroll along the wind-blown sands of that far-off land and cry out, "O God, let me hear from you—let me know your will—show me your next move!" But for months there was no word, no clear command from Christ. Only the great, quiet stillness of the ocean edge—only the wash of the waves on the sand—only the cry of the sea birds in the wind.

Had God forsaken me? No! Had the Lord forgotten me? No! Was he being unfaithful to his servant? No! He was allowing me to be refreshed and rested for the great events soon to follow.

Likewise this was true for Elijah.

Suddenly one day the word of the Lord came to him, emphatically, clearly, powerfully.

Elijah Complies with God's Command

"Go and confront Ahab again!"

"Challenge this diabolical monarch!"

"Meet this monster face to face without fear!"

Elijah was ready for that command. He was a man waiting for a signal from heaven. He did not flinch or hesitate a moment. He was completely combat ready and moved into action at once. It was what he had been waiting for. The time to challenge the forces of evil again had come.

Suddenly now, he would burst out of the obscurity of the wings to leap full force onto the center stage of Israel's tempestuous drama. The events of the next few days would be a dramatic turnabout not only for Elijah but also for all of his nation.

It is the person who has been in the quiet place, alone with God, who is going to have a message from the Lord. If any person is to have power with men and God, he has to derive that energy and thrust from personal, intimate contact with Christ. Elijah had. He was a man charged for combat.

Elijah was fully conditioned for the confrontation on Carmel. Again and again he had responded positively to the commands of God. It was what fitted him for the fray. We simply must see that he was a man under command.

He had dared to defy Ahab the first time.

He had fearlessly predicted and called for a famine.

He had calmly accepted the cutting ordeal at Cherith.

He had humbly received the hospitality of a widow.

He had quietly waited more than three years for God's next command.

Now he was a man equipped to move with might.

It mattered not to Elijah that for him to confront Ahab again was to literally walk into the very jaws of death. The instant he showed himself, Jezebel would expend her full force and fury to liquidate him. As far as she and her awful Ahab were concerned Elijah was public enemy number one. He was the cause of all their calamities. He was the one who forecast the famine. He was the one who troubled Israel.

But the word that came to Elijah from the Lord did not just concern him. It related to all of Israel, all of Samaria, the capital of Ahab's kingdom, and all of the false gods that had become ensconced in the country under Jezebel's perfidious power.

There would be rain!

The drought would be broken.

The famine would end.

The land would be refreshed and restored to productivity.

God's word to Elijah was—"*I will send rain upon the earth*."

This was to be God's act, not Baal's.

This was to be Jehovah's intervention, not that of the false storm god.

This was to be the display of the Lord's might in response to the faith and faithfulness of his chosen servant Elijah.

One man with God would prove to be a majority, even though Israel was plagued with hundreds of false prophets.

There is a profound and powerful lesson for us of the twentieth century to learn here. Insidiously many of us are succumbing to the world's view and the false idea that our destiny lies in the hands of science and technology. We are being brainwashed to believe just as blatantly as the Israelis were by the false prophets of Baal. We are led to believe our future depends upon the skill, expertise and manipulative powers of man. We insist that given enough men, enough money, enough hours of research and experiment we can come up with answers to the human dilemma.

It is a dreadful delusion.

It is an atheistic deception.

In our day, just as in Elijah's day, it is ultimately God who will decide and decree what shall happen on planet earth. World climate, inter-planetary movements, the shift of continental plates, and the colossal action of ocean currents are all beyond the capacity of man to manipulate. Their action is decided in the providential counsel of our God. It is he who ultimately condescends to let the rain fall upon the just and unjust. His sun shines on both saint and sinner. And in that profound awareness we are well advised to walk humbly before him.

God's word to Elijah was that rain would come.

Not only had there been a dreadful drought to dry up the springs and streams; to parch and bake the land; to shrivel crops and destroy pasturage; to starve animals and reduce people to terrible privation; but also there had been an appalling dearth of God's word in Israel. There had been no spiritual refreshment for more than three long years.

The prophets of the Lord had been silenced.

No altar to Jehovah remained anywhere in Israel.

Sacrifice to God had come to an end.

So the rain which Elijah knew was in the offing now was more than just water to refresh the land. It was a word from God to restore the spirit of his people. Elijah would bring more than just rain. He would also bring revival by his obedience.

1 Kings 18:3–8

8

Elijah Meets Obadiah

When Elijah returned from Zarephath to meet Ahab his initial encounter was with the king's chamberlain, Obadiah. This man was the most highly placed civil servant in Samaria. He was, in fact, next in rank to the king himself. He had full responsibility for governing and administering all the affairs of the royal household. And this of course, also included complying with all the wishes of both Ahab and his crafty queen Jezebel.

Obadiah stands in Scripture as one of the most baffling and bewildering of all characters. On the one hand he obviously held the wicked, evil Ahab, whom he served so well, in enormous respect. Yet on the other hand the record reports that he also held the Lord God, Jehovah, in great reverence. For when the cruel, violent Jezebel set out to exterminate all the prophets of God, Obadiah had skillfully sheltered a hundred of them in subterranean caves. Perhaps they were placed in the great underground quarries beneath Jerusalem where Solomon's stone masons had hewn out the giant blocks for building his magnificent temple.

There are some who feel that Obadiah represents to us the so-called "secret Christian." That, like Nicodemus in our Lord's day, he was active behind the scenes, serving the cause of God in whatever small way he could. Yet, he was never bold enough to make a real break with his ties to the old life. Strange as it sounds the name *Obadiah* means "servant of God." And even stranger was the reliance put upon him by his master Ahab.

For Ahab had decided that at the height of the dreadful drought now destroying all of Samaria, he and Obadiah would give up their search for Elijah, public enemy number one, and go instead in search of whatever bit of green grass they could find around remaining streams and springs. This would at least insure that some of the king's horses and mules would survive.

So for the first time, perhaps the only time, in all his years of servitude to Ahab, the loyal Obadiah was out on his own, away from his monarch searching and scouring the sun-burned countryside for grass. The two men had mutually agreed to divide the whole of Ahab's kingdom between them, each going in a different direction to try and find pasturage for the royal horses and mules.

Obviously green grass had become an absolute priority both in Ahab and Obadiah's estimation. This is what completely dominated all their energies and attention at this moment in time. Both top ranking rulers in the land had made pasturage their first consideration.

During the long, hot, tedious treks from water spring to water hole, to drying up stream bed, Obadiah mused about the dreadful plight of the countryside. The whole land was slowly but surely dying. Water sources were drying up, and water supplies were dwindling. Streams were becoming nothing but dry trenches of sun-baked boulders and dry sand. Trees, bushes, shrubs and grass were withered. Some had died in the drought. Grass, long since gnawed into the ground, in places even pawed out of the hot soil to have its roots consumed by ruinous sheep and goats, had become more precious than gold, as rare as an emerald gemstone.

Why, why? Why had this happened to his homeland?

A thousand conflicting causes must have raced and raged through Obadiah's thoughts. Was it just because of Elijah? Was it because of Ahab's evil ways? Was it God's judgment on Jezebel? Or was it simply because all of Israel had long since forsaken her God Jehovah? Could one be sure? Was there any simple answer?

Then suddenly one day as Obadiah was on his way to find yet another waterhole where some grass might grow for his master's mules, he came face to face with Elijah!

It was a terribly confusing encounter for the lord chamberlain. The last person he ever expected to see again was the powerful prophet from the desert. He simply could not believe his eyes.

Instantly the richly attired governor recognized Elijah. After all it was he who had ushered the flaming firebrand into Ahab's august presence more than three years before. He had then stood by his monarch in somber silence, listening awestruck and spell-bound to the prophet's momentous prediction, "*As the Lord God of Israel liveth, before whom I stand, there shall not be dew nor rain these years, but according to my word*" (1 Kings 17:1).

The syllables had come from the fearsome prophet like flashes of lightning and ominous bolts of thunder. They shook Ahab. They startled Jezebel. They sobered Obadiah.

Then Obadiah had escorted Elijah out of the king's royal rooms. Like the last breath of rising mist the desert spokesman had simply vanished into the haze and heat of the awful drought. And now for more than three long years he had been lost to view. All of the palace police, all the special spies, all the undercover agents appointed by Ahab to arrest Elijah had never been able to turn up a single clue as to his whereabouts.

Surely he was a mystery man!

Perhaps like Enoch of old, God had simply taken him away. Or indeed, as with Moses, maybe he had been buried by God on some remote, obscure mountain peak unknown to man.

But no, here Elijah stood, in living reality, blood, bone and flesh, looking him full in the face.

Obadiah was overwhelmed. In utter obeisance he fell to his knees, bowing low before the prophet.

"*Art thou that my lord Elijah?*" (1 Kings 18:7).

"*Are you really my lord—my prophet—my divine advocate—Elijah?*"

Obadiah's mind could scarcely credit what his eyes saw.

It was an impossible miracle.

Elijah surely was not still at large!

But he was, and his prompt reply to Obadiah shattered the governor's poise. "*I am Elijah. I am alive. I am here. Go and tell your lord Ahab.*"

It was the toughest assignment Obadiah had ever been given. No longer could he play his cozy games of being a secret believer.

It may be appropriate to say that Obadiah is given to us in God's Word more as an example of a carnal Christian than a secret believer. It was Elijah who finally forced this vacillating character to make a decisive choice as to who really was his Lord. He had called Elijah his lord, yet the prophet in turn had insisted that it was really King Ahab who was the governor's lord.

Obadiah had never fully resolved the conflict of interests in his own life between serving God and serving Ahab. He had tried unsuccessfully to make the most of both worlds. He had, to put it in the contemporary colloquialism of our times, tried to play both ends of the field against the middle. He tried to shelter himself by serving both masters—Ahab and God.

Tragically he had not succeeded, sincere as his intentions may have been. When he hid the hundred prophets, using his good office and influence to spare their lives, he really had not achieved any great gain. For their voices and testimony had been as strictly silenced during that time in Israel as if they had in fact been buried by Jezebel.

And even though Obadiah had served as Ahab's first minister, his testimony was so impoverished and his witness so weak, that in no way had he ever deterred his monarch from doing evil. If anything, he had become an accomplice with Ahab and Jezebel in their diabolical deeds, for silence gives both consent and tacit endorsement to any action it does not oppose.

Obviously Obadiah had never opened his mouth in outright protest against the wickedness of his master. He had never taken a tough stand for what was right. Every move he made was designed and planned to protect his own position—to feather his own nest.

With his keen, sharp, spiritual intuition, Elijah saw through the governor's duplicity. He knew Obadiah was riding the fence with divided affections and divided loyalties. The time had come to call his bluff. Whom did he really serve? His Lord God Jehovah or his lord Ahab and Queen Jezebel?

For Obadiah it was the moment of truth. Where did he stand? And all of us might well ask ourselves, "Where do I stand? Whom do I serve?"

Often in life God arranges for us to have a firsthand encounter with one of his own chosen people whom we can no longer fool by our piety. He allows our path to cross that of one of his prophets. It may be a man or woman who truly walks with God, in whom the Spirit of God resides in generous plenitude. And when we meet them we know of a surety that we are meeting Christ in personal confrontation.

The playacting is suddenly all over. The false front and pious pretense are dropped. The folly of fooling around with our loyalties is ended. We are face to face with truth. The time to come clean has arrived. Will we or won't we respond to the Word of God, the self-revelation of himself and ourselves?

Obadiah's private encounter with Elijah floored him. He may have been able to fool Ahab for years—but not this prophet of power. In and through Elijah he was in contact with the Living Lord.

This God, through his spokesman, calls us to face truth. He offers the choice of giving ourselves to him or to the world around us. We cannot be people of divided minds, divided loyalties, divided affections.

The truth is that many of us do know what is proper and appropriate for us to do. But like Obadiah we are rather reluctant to commit ourselves to acting bravely on God's behalf. We prefer to play it safe. Unsuccessfully we try to accommodate ourselves both to the social culture of our times and to truth as revealed to us in God's Word.

Truth does not in fact become viable, potent and powerful in our lives until it is actually acted out. It is otherwise only a hypothetical credence—an insipid "believism."

But the instant an individual steps out to *live truth—to do God's will—to comply with Christ's commands*—it becomes to him both spirit and supernatural life: The life of God himself. This Elijah knew and experienced.

It was something still unknown, obscure, foreign to the bland fickle Obadiah.

9

Obadiah's Objections and Obedience

Elijah's command to Obadiah that he report to Ahab at once that public enemy number one had been found seemed both drastic and devastating to the governor. The simple reason was that Obadiah was sure the moment he left Elijah's presence, the prophet would be borne away into hiding again by the Spirit of God.

Then, when he could not be found, his own head would be forfeit under the fury of Ahab's anger. After all, Ahab and Jezebel had left no stone unturned to try to capture the elusive Elijah. All of the forces at their command had been thrown into a frantic search for the desert firebrand. For three long years their intricate network of spies that sought Elijah both at home and abroad had come back empty handed—thwarted at every turn.

Nation after nation had sworn to Ahab that they were not providing sanctuary or safety to the elusive prophet. No doubt even the Sidonians in their ignorance had assured Ahab and Jezebel that Elijah was not there.

Yet here, now, the powerful prophet had accosted the king's chamberlain and commanded that he boldly reveal his whereabouts. Obadiah was absolutely sure the whole arrangement was a bit of intrigue to trap him. He was sure this was a maneuver that would cost him his very life.

Suddenly Obadiah developed a grim guilt complex. He sensed that at last his own duplicity in trying to serve two masters, both the Lord and Ahab, had caught up with him. Vehemently he protested his innocence to Elijah. Did he not know, had he not heard, how when Jezebel set out to slay all the prophets of God, he Obadiah, had hidden a hundred of them in a cave?

Didn't Elijah know that from his boyhood he had feared Jehovah and endeavored to show him great reverence? Why, then, should he be exposed to this sudden, extreme danger of dying under Ahab's wrath if he failed to produce the prophet? What had he done wrong to deserve such unfair treatment?

Obadiah's strong protests and strong objections to obeying the word of the Lord through Elijah clearly disclosed the duplicity and double dealing of his own character. It was a dead giveaway.

First of all it was obvious Obadiah really did not completely trust either Elijah or Elijah's God. He was not at all sure they could be counted on in the crisis that now confronted him. Nor did he trust Ahab whom he had served so dutifully for so many years. He felt uneasy about the king's angry reaction in this ticklish situation.

So in reality Obadiah found himself in a frightening bind. He was caught between the upper and nether millstones of a spiritual monarch and an earthly king, both of whom he had tried to serve in fear, but neither of whom he totally followed. In his cunning craftiness Obadiah had tried to cover all the angles in his career.

Now suddenly in the intense light and burning presence of the desert prophet, all his defenses were destroyed. He stood stripped, exposed and extremely vulnerable.

He was, to use a New Testament phrase uttered by John in the book of Revelation, neither hot or cold but lukewarm.

Obadiah is portrayed for us in vivid colors as a carnal Christian. He is the person who is very much in the world, a devotee of the world, a man who with skill and craftiness has accommodated himself to the world's reprehensible ways. Such a one has enjoyed a certain degree of success and acceptance in the world. He has achieved power, prestige and position there without ever really endangering himself. Yet all the time, deep down, he knows instinctively that the world and its people really cannot be fully trusted. His loyalty at best is shallow and superficial.

At the same time the carnal Christian is also trying his utmost to make it with God. He feels, somehow, that if he can do some good deeds, perhaps even put himself out a little for the Lord, it will all be credited to his account in the heavenly ledgers. So in the long run there will be something to cushion him against any calamities which may occur in life.

He fears God. He is sure he is an august Judge who holds him accountable for his conduct. He really does not either love or adore the Lord. He never really considers him as a friend. At best all his life he has had only a rather remote, respectful, rather nodding acquaintance with God. He does not wish to become too intimately acquainted lest there be demands made upon him which would jeopardize his cozy accommodation with the world. To be moved by great love for Christ is unknown to him.

In truth, though he claims to serve both man and God, he actually does neither, but lives only to serve his own selfish, self-centered best interests. He is concerned primarily only with his own survival. Above all else he wants only his own security.

Such individuals the Spirit of God finds reprehensible. They are neither hot nor cold. They are nauseating.

And it was so between Elijah and Obadiah.

Elijah simply could not stand Obadiah's vacillation. He adamantly refused to accept any of his objections.

A second time he reiterated in powerful language that could not be misunderstood: *"As the Lord of hosts liveth, before whom I stand, I will surely show myself unto him today"* (Kings 18:15). His words drove Obadiah to act.

Of course Obadiah may have had a secret fear that if he reported to Ahab that he had found Elijah, it would be construed that he knew all along where the prophet had been in hiding. Obadiah may have been terrified that Ahab suspected him of sheltering Elijah, just as he had sheltered the other hundred prophets. If so, then naturally his life would be forfeit. It was a terrible risk to go back and report to Ahab that Elijah was waiting to meet the evil monarch again.

But something profound and strangely moving took place in the vacillating soul of Obadiah that drastic day. For the first time faith—simple forthright faith, a positive response to Elijah's reassurance of his own reliability in God—was expressed in the governor's conduct.

Taking his life in his own hands he hurried off to find Ahab and tell him Elijah had returned. What was more, Elijah was waiting to meet him in that very same spot. Suddenly finding grass for mules and horses was not a priority.

The impact of Obadiah's report was sufficient to compel Ahab to come and confront his opponent. Something about the sincerity, earnestness and intensity of Obadiah's obedience to Elijah's command had repercussions in the royal household. Ahab, as king, did not insist that Elijah be brought before him, but rather he went to meet the man of God.

The influence and power of God was being felt already in the evil heart of Ahab simply because of Obadiah's compliance with the word of the Lord through Elijah. Like a pebble dropped in a still pond, the ever widening circle of ripples would spread out from this small epicenter to touch the whole life of the entire nation of Israel.

God is ever searching, seeking, surveying the souls of men and women to find here and there someone who might be open and available to his plans and purposes for them. He had found such a one at last in the reluctant, double-minded Obadiah. Through him Ahab and Elijah were again to meet. It would prove to be the prelude to the mighty events to follow on Mount Carmel.

The Lord is always using any means possible to get carnal Christians off the fence. He is looking for those who will come down hard on his side. He is waiting to use any man and woman willing to risk themselves for him. He can and will take the most unlikely people to achieve great things. For once they have invested their faith and confidence in him, he does the rest in his own wondrous way. Obadiah's obedience was a part of the great victory to come on Carmel.

10

Elijah Challenges Ahab

Like a small, belligerent terrier snapping at a giant Alsatian that has come into his domain, Ahab literally launched himself in angry vituperation against Elijah. Snarling and yapping furiously he hurled abuse upon the powerful prophet.

"So you are the trouble maker in Israel! You are the one who has brought this dreadful drought upon us. You are to blame for the awful famine!"

It was a cruel charge that could come only from an evil man well nigh demented by his own diabolical designs. Ahab and Jezebel were monsters. The Middle East has a habit of spawning such families. Roughly 900 years later the terrible Herods would come to power in Israel. They, like Ahab and Jezebel, would be murderers and butchers of innocent people. In cold blood they would cut down any whom they felt might even remotely threaten their throne.

Ahab and Jezebel had already liquidated all the prophets of God in Israel, and at this point they were prepared to take off Elijah's head as well.

But Elijah was not to be intimidated by Ahab's diatribe. He had been sent by God to stand before the atrocious monarch. He would face his fury without flinching. Instead of retreating he would turn the tables and bring the swaggering bully to bay with a fierce barrage of powerful imprecations.

His eyes flaming from beneath his bushy brows, his voice low and even, but packed with power, Elijah looked directly at Ahab and retorted.

"It is not I who has troubled Israel, but you. Both you and your family before you have chosen deliberately to forsake the laws of the Lord. And instead you have followed the falsehood of Baal!"

It was an indisputable indictment.

It was a straightforward statement of fact.

It was a declaration that could not be denied or debated.

It was simply so!

The significant thing was that Ahab made no move to defend his deeds. He did not even try to explain his actions. He realized that in one slashing attack the fierce desert firebrand had torn away his façade, and now he stood fully exposed in his evil. The fault for all the famine and terrible suffering lay with him and not with Elijah.

It is noteworthy that Ahab had never launched any attack against Obadiah, even though the latter was ostensibly also supposed to be a servant of God. Somehow the two had come to a cozy mutual accommodation. It is often that way between the world and carnal Christians.

But the instant a true man of God stepped onto the stage of Israel's public life, Ahab's anger against Elijah flared to white heat.

Evil and good are mutually exclusive.

Corruption and purity are not compatible.

Righteousness and wrongdoing polarize each other.

Falsehood and truth repel one another.

As God's people we simply have to see this. Paul put

it bluntly in 2 Timothy 3:12, when he wrote to young Timothy, *"All that will live godly in Christ Jesus shall suffer persecution."* Our Lord declared to his disciples just before his death on the cross, *"If they* [the world] *have persecuted me, they will also persecute you"* (John 15:20).

The world is forever looking for someone upon whom they can pin the blame for the disasters that overtake them. If it is not God himself who is charged with their calamities, then it is God's people who are held responsible. This is especially true if Christians are bold enough to stand for the truth. If, like Elijah, they are courageous enough to come out openly and declare that it is men who have gone wrong and thus brought evil upon themselves, there will be a critical confrontation.

It is one of the eternal, inviolate, invincible principles of divine origin that any individual, any family, any community, any nation that knows what is right, but refuses to do it, will undergo enormous suffering. One does not ignore the good will of God with impunity. No one can repudiate and reject the right conduct of a gracious, loving, caring God and not face utter disaster.

It is not that God is vindictive, a cruel tyrant. He is not one to delight in the destruction of evil wrongdoers. To have and hold such a view of him is erroneous.

The profound truth is this. Every law, every edict, every command, every guideline for proper and appropriate behavior given to men by God has been bestowed upon us for our own well being and prosperity. He always has only our own best interests in mind.

The man or woman, family or nation that flaunts those laws; who repudiates and rejects them willfully;

who "breaks them" with impunity, discovers to their sorrow that it is not the laws of God which are actually broken, but themselves.

And it was this principle with which Elijah challenged Ahab on the critical occasion before us.

Ahab's forbears and family, beginning with Jeroboam and Omri, then Ahab himself, had rejected the goodness of God. In violent disregard for the commandments of Jehovah they had led Israel into deception and debauchery. The whole nation was sold out to the false gods of Baal and Ashteroth. Their whole society was rotten with immorality, greed, violence, and malicious materialism. They were a people now mired in the muck of man-made humanism. So the time had come for God to declare and show himself strong again.

There is an important lesson here for us of the Western world. At our own peril do we repudiate and reject the noble heritage given to us by our forefathers under God. If as a nation or people we deliberately break his commands, time will show that it is in truth those inviolate laws which crush and reduce us to dust as a once great nation under God.

Elijah was not content just to charge Ahab with the calamities that had overwhelmed Israel. He wanted a fierce, face-to-face confrontation with all the false prophets of the heathen gods who had victimized his people.

He challenged Ahab to summon all the devotees of Baal and Ashteroth to the summit of Carmel. There had gradually proliferated a whole crowd of these contemptible characters in the community life of Israel. Like a malignant cancer they had spread and penetrated to every part of the country. Some 450 of Baal's false spokesmen had insinuated themselves into the life of Elijah's beloved nation. And there were at least 400 equally despicable parasites who pandered to

Ashteroth living off the larder given them by the vicious Jezebel—a crafty queen determined to destroy the last vestige of Jehovah's influence in Israel.

Elijah was determined to exorcise and eradicate all the evil forces at work in his beloved homeland in a single daring, dramatic confrontation. He had been away for three long, slow, grinding years. During his absence the voice of God had been silenced in Israel. The underground activities of Baal and Ashteroth had surfaced to subvert the entire nation. No altar remained standing upon which sacrifices were offered to the Lord. Instead, the lewd licentiousness of temple prostitutes, both men and women, had proliferated everywhere, leading Israel down into utter degradation and bestiality. Sacred groves were planted everywhere. Here sexual orgies and atrocious perversion were practiced with impunity. Modern pornography has nothing new that Israel had not already tried and tasted 2,800 years ago.

She was a nation in a slime pit of sensuality. She simply had to be delivered from utter destruction.

Elijah, under God, was determined that this could happen at Carmel. It would seem the choice of such a picturesque and pleasant site was inappropriate, but he had chosen this location for the confrontation for a very special reason.

Mount Carmel with its magnificent setting overlooking the blue Mediterranean was the most favored and fruitful spot in the whole of Palestine. Here, close to the sea, its climate tempered and caressed by the mist of the sea breezes, it enjoyed beautiful mild weather. Even during the dreadful drought Carmel had not suffered as severely as other less fortunate parts of the parched country.

On Carmel the soil, too, was unusually rich and productive. For uncounted centuries it had been tilled and tended with special care. Here all sorts of crops grew to perfection in the salubrious climate. If Baal's claim to be the god of fruitfulness and fertility could be demonstrated anywhere it was on the crest of this magnificent mount.

The devotees of Baal and Ashteroth may have had real problems convincing the common people that they controlled weather and crop production in the more impoverished and drought-ridden areas of Palestine. But that would never be so on Carmel. There everything was in their favor. So with cunning consent Ahab agreed to summon all the false prophets of his false gods to the spot where he was most confident they could call down rain.

It is a mark of Elijah's enormous faith in God that the prophet did not even reconsider the choice of site for the divine duel. He could well have protested that Ahab was gaining an unfair advantage since Carmel was the great bastion of Baal. He could well have insisted that since he himself was a son of the desert wastes, and he stood alone against some 850 of the false prophets of Baal and Ashteroth, at least he should have the benefit of choosing the trysting ground in some rather grim and gaunt desert location.

But to his credit Elijah did not debate this issue.

He would come to Carmel.

He would confront Ahab and his cohorts there.

He would call upon all Israel to witness the contest.

His confidence would be in the Lord to conquer the enemy and confirm his power.

11

Elijah Challenges Israel and Her False Prophets

In response to Ahab's edict that the entire nation should assemble on Mount Carmel for a spiritual showdown, people gathered there from all over the country. They came in crowds, curious to see what the powerful prophet, who alone still survived the onslaughts of Jezebel, had to say.

But it was more than mere curiosity that brought the masses to this mount. Israel, this peculiar people chosen of God for his own special purposes, was in a crisis. It was not only an economic and social crisis created by the cruel three-year famine that had flattened the land, but also a spiritual crisis in which the voice of the Lord had been stilled. The altars of Jehovah had been flattened as well. The sacred flame of fire for sacrifice had been quenched. There was a dreadful dearth of spiritual sustenance for Israel's spirit. The soul of her people was as impoverished as the parched fields of her land.

Fearless, formidable, fierce for the glory and honor of his God, Elijah did not hesitate to stand alone under the blazing sun challenging his countrymen. At the top of his lungs he shouted to them from the summit of the mount. His eyes blazed with fire. His voice rolled like the drums of impending doom.

"How long—how long, O Israel, are you going to stagger and stumble between two loyalties? If Jehovah the Lord be God then follow him. If Baal be God, then give him your full allegiance!"

It was a stabbing statement. It was a cutting commentary on the nation's conduct. It was a crucial question that touched the very heart of Israel's crisis.

For 585 years this wayward, willful, stiff-necked, stubborn nation had vacillated like wind-driven waves in their allegiance to the Lord. Since the days of their deliverance out of Egypt under the flaming leadership of Moses, they had been a people of divided minds, divided emotions, and divided loyalties. Again and again they had turned to follow the false gods of the pagan people around them. Over and over God had sent them judges, generals, prophets and priests to bring them back from the brink of total destruction.

How longsuffering, how patient, how persistent, how generous the Lord had been. If he had dealt with them in direct proportion to their misdeeds, Israel would long since have been allowed to perish as a people and pass into oblivion.

Again on this sun-drenched mount, through his special servant, God was appealing to this awkward, hard-hearted people to repent and turn to him. But their response to the flaming challenge of the fiery prophet was utter silence. They simply stared at him as if oblivious to his cry. Their indifference was as dry as the drought that held their land in its deadly grip. They could not care less.

Elijah shouted at them a second time. *"I alone remain as a spokesman for the Lord! This is your very last chance, O Israel, to hear from heaven. You have 450 false prophets of Baal who will lead you astray."*

The people were being forced to face facts. Elijah was not afraid to stand alone. He did not hesitate to become a marked man. The prophet had a message from God for these fickle, wavering multitudes. He had stepped out of the total obscurity of Cherith and Zarephath onto the center stage of Israel's public life. He would be heard. He would be seen. He would show that his God, whom he served, and before whom he stood, was God very God.

The personal hazards didn't count.

The danger to his own life did not matter.

There was a message from God to deliver to this decadent people. And he would do it at any cost.

The mob may well have been in a mood to lynch him. The false prophets of Baal would have been glad to put a sword between his ribs.

But Elijah was God's man, in God's place, in God's time. No power in heaven or earth could touch him. This he knew. And in this assurance he pressed the point of his challenge even further.

If Israel would not respond to mere words, perhaps they would react to real action. If there was a demonstration of divine power, and the divine presence of the very person of God, amongst them their spiritual lethargy would be stirred and stimulated.

In bold, blazing faith Elijah threw down the gauntlet of ultimate challenge. It was an audacious act which none could ignore. "*Bring out two bullocks. One for me, one for the prophets of Baal. Each of us will butcher a beast; lay it upon wood on a prepared altar, and appeal to our respective gods to send down fire to consume the sacrifice. The God who does, be it Baal or Jehovah, is God indeed!*"

The immediate response from the audience was electrifying, dramatic and surprising. "*Well said—well said!*" they shouted and screamed. "*Let it be so.*"

Perhaps a little drama, a bit of action, a spiritual duel, if you wish, would brighten up their day. After all, they were by now a nation steeped in sexual orgies and licentious displays. They were a people sotted with counterfeit spiritual activities. False gods, false prophets, false sacrifices, false priorities, false life styles, false leaders, false beliefs had formed the fabric of life in Israel in recent years.

As far as they were concerned just one more dramatic display in the name of God couldn't possibly do any harm. Cynically they thought, "Bring on the gods. Let them indulge their gory, gruesome games. We will watch their showmanship. We will decide who puts on the best performance. What a lark! What a show! Anything to pass another boring day in the drudgery of this dreadful drought."

Little was Israel prepared for a true visitation from God that day. Before the desert stars shone clear and bright that night they would see with shocked eyes and trembling hearts what God could do. But at this point it was all still just a little game—or so they thought.

There is a powerful parallel and stirring similarity between Israel in Elijah's day and our own society in this late twentieth century. All the main ingredients of a similar drama are there. The main pieces of the same play are present. History in the human story simply keeps repeating its act over and over.

We of the West are a people who once walked with God in a rather unique and special way. We knew what it was to have our trust in him. We were a society who in great part knew and recognized the rule and government of God in our affairs.

Gradually across the years false gods and false prophets and false philosophies have insinuated themselves into the very fabric of our culture. Eastern religions, false cults, the occult, humanism, outright sexual perversion, violence and total preoccupation with materialism and affluence have all become powerful influences at work in the lives of our people.

The servants of God cry out to us to turn from our wicked ways. The Word of the Lord is proclaimed loudly. The prophets amongst us plead for us to be done with our wavering between God and the world. We are challenged to follow Christ in total commitment. Yet so often the response is a lethargic indifference. People don't really care. They are sotted with the world's ways.

On the other hand some are ready, eager and anxious to see some dramatic display. They seek some special miracle or far-out fire from heaven to come into action as proof that God is really around. And it matters not who it may be that offers to bring down fire; they will follow them. It may be the false prophets of Baal or it may be a true touch from God.

Man has always been intrigued by divine pyrotechnics: Be they true or false, counterfeit or genuine in their origin.

What Israel seemed to have missed this day was the deep significance of the sort of sacrifice upon which Elijah had insisted. They were totally preoccupied with the fire. They were fascinated with the idea of flames.

It is noteworthy Elijah demanded that a bullock, an ox, be butchered. He did not request a lamb, a kid, a bushel of grain or a pair of doves. He insisted on a bullock. Therein lies the key and secret to all that was later to take place on this mount on this monumental day.

A priest, a prophet, a man of God, offered an ox in sacrifice to God only for his own special, private sins and wrongdoing. It was an atonement made on behalf of just himself and his own immediate household.

The sincere, implicit offering of a bullock declared to God his own awareness of his own unworthiness. This was a sacred rite instituted by God himself for the cleansing and purification and preparation of his own servants. It recognized that even a man like Elijah, like Aaron of old, like Samuel, had need of proper preparation in spirit, soul and body to stand as an intermediary between God and man.

> And Aaron shall offer his bullock of the sin offering, which is for himself, and make an atonement for himself, and for his house (Lev. 16:6).

The bullock was a sin offering. It showed that the true in heart must be made right always with God in utter humility and complete contrition.

Always, ever, it is the person humble in mind, broken in heart, contrite in spirit with whom God, by his Spirit, deigns to come and dwell. He delights to come and touch the spirit of the man who sees himself undone before him. He draws near to the one who senses his sin, seeks cleansing, and believes implicitly that he will come to abide.

None of this was true of the prophets of Baal. None of them ever saw his need of a savior.

But Elijah did. Despite all of the great deeds done on his behalf by God, this humble servant still knew his own unworthiness. So when he prayed his requests would be honored. God always honors those who honor him.

12

False Gods without Answers

Just as Elijah had been most generous in agreeing to confront the gods of Baal and Ashteroth on Carmel, so now he was equally generous in granting their false prophets first chance to call down fire from above. The powerful prophet was determined to demonstrate beyond any doubt that only the Lord Jehovah was truly alive. In daring faith he granted his opponents every possible advantage in the contest.

"You go first. There are so many more of you. Take your time. You've got all day. Offer the ox of your own choice to your own gods. Sacrifice it to Baal. Lay it on ample wood. But light no fire. Call on your gods to consume it."

The conditions were generous yet also demanding. Elijah knew full well that the sacred flame of God's own divine appointment and presence had been extinguished by Ahab and Jezebel. With the execution of all the Israelite prophets, and the substitution of pagan worship in Israel, the altars of sacrifice to Jehovah had been broken down and their perpetual fires quenched.

It had been ordained of God when Israel was delivered out of Egypt that the celestial fires of sacrifice ignited upon her altars should never be allowed to die.

The fire shall ever be burning upon the altar; it shall never go out (Lev. 6:13).

But the fire of God's presence; the fire of God's power; the fire of God's promises to his people had gone out. There was no longer any public worship. There was no longer any penitence and sacrifice for sin in the life of this proud, perverse and petulant nation. There was no longer the presence of God himself manifest to lead, guide and govern this stiff-necked, stubborn people.

Again there would need to be divine intervention from above. Again God would have to manifest himself in reality to this indifferent race. Again it was time for a touch of fire from heaven.

There was no doubt in Elijah's spirit that God would do this when he offered his own evening sacrifice for sin. God had accepted the sacrifices of sincere souls from the very beginning of time. Over and over in the history of Israel the Lord had consumed the sacrifices of his saints, which they offered to him in humility and honesty. The sacred flame had come down upon the altars of Abraham, Aaron, Gideon and Manoah. It would come down on Elijah's altar at Carmel.

But by the same measure Elijah was equally sure that if any sort of false fire was set under the sacrifice terrible consequences could occur. Men, apart from God, who dabbled in counterfeit religion could ignite false fire that would be both destructive and demonic. It had happened in the case of Nadab and Abihu. In pride and arrogance they had offered strange fire of their own origin before the Lord and it spelled instant death (read Lev. 10:1–7).

What was true in Moses' day was still true in Elijah's

day, and remains true today. Yet, strange as it may seem, there are those who are not averse to playing with the false fire of counterfeit cults, false religions and even the occult. Modern man is becoming obsessed by a preoccupation with so-called "fire from heaven." It matters not what its source or origin may be. It seems to make no difference whether it is truly of a divine or demonic nature. As long as their insatiable propensity for inflammatory experiences is satisfied, men pray for fire, expect fire, look for fire and boast of fire—be it ever so false.

To Elijah's credit he insisted that not even the false prophets of the false gods had either the privilege or prerogative to place their own peculiar fire under the sacrifice. It simply would not do. It was no substitute for a true touch from the Lord Jehovah.

We do well to ponder this point. It is a most sobering and serious consideration in the church worldwide. What are we looking for? A counterfeit conflagration—or God's presence?

From morning until high noon the host of the false prophets pranced around the altar they had erected. They prostrated themselves before the sacrifice, lying in great slabs upon the pile of dry wood. They pleaded and cried to Baal, their god of thunderstorms, hail, rain and lightning, to flash down and ignite the fuel they had placed upon the altar. One simple stroke of lightning on the summit of Carmel was all they needed to ignite the wood, split the rocks and consume the carcass.

But the skies remained clear, cloudless, a brittle blue. Not a hint of a thundercloud lifted above the horizon. Not a single sign of any impending storm cast its shadow over the mount. Not a single cumulus thunderhead developed in which lightning would be generated to go flashing and crashing down to Mount Carmel.

Instead, only a swarm of sinister flies, drawn by the blood, flesh and offal of the sacrifice hovered over the carcass. The flies crawled over the meat until it appeared blackened by their hordes. And in the sky overhead hungry vultures and scavenging ravens wheeled in great circles on dark wings, waiting for a feast of flesh.

Elijah, a bit bored by the whole performance of the false prophets, decided to draw near and taunt them: *"Shout louder. Call harder. Perhaps your god is busy in conversation. Maybe he is away on a trip. Perhaps he has fallen asleep. Awaken him to answer you!"*

It was not only Elijah who mocked them. Even worse it was their own gods who mocked them. Ahab saw this and so did the multitudes of common people who had gathered to witness the contest. The false gods of Baal and Ashteroth could come up with no answers to the cries and pleas of their adherents. The excited, frantic, deluded prophets were being double-crossed. The whole thing was a pathetic performance.

The false gods of Baal and Ashteroth had given not only their prophets, but all other worshipers false hope, false aspirations, false expectations.

The gods of this world always do that. It matters not whether those gods be something as absurd and stupid as a chunk of cedar carved into an idol or as sophisticated as a humanistic philosophy based only on human reason.

The world has always been plagued with a plethora of false and futile gods. They run the full gamut from something as sordid as a slab of stone chiseled by a pagan stonecutter into the shape of a serpent, to the most intricate and elaborate occult rites devised under devilish design, suggested by the old "serpent" himself.

Multitudes upon uncounted multitudes of men and women, deluded in their darkness, have followed and fallen for the falsehood of false gods and their false prophets.

In my own lifetime we were told the following falsehoods in each decade. Here they are:

In the titillating 1920s—*Education* has all the answers.

In the "dirty" 1930s—*Economics* has all the answers.

In the formidable 1940s—*Politics* and *peace* have all the answers.

In the fantastic 1950s—*Science* has all the answers.

In the soaring 1960s—*Sociology* has all the answers.

In the sizzling 1970s—*Hedonism* has all the answers.

We have lived through all these eras to witness all their prophets shout and scream that with them are to be found answers to life's enigma. And yet each has mocked and betrayed its followers. In none of them have adequate answers been found to satisfy a searching, stumbling society, as it staggers down the road to ultimate ruin.

Even the most ardent proponents of the false gods have begun to doubt the reliability of their gods. It matters not whether they be educators, economists, politicians, scientists, sociologists, or sensual religious fanatics. Each in his own way is as frustrated as the false prophets leaping on their altar on Mount Carmel.

The hot, sun-burned, heat-scorched day dragged on. The noise of the shouting, screaming, wailing prophets rose to an ear-deafening crescendo. They chanted their prayers. They gesticulated wildly with their arms and legs. They grimaced with their faces. Some in the extreme frenzy of their fanaticism slashed their own bodies with knives and daggers. Blood oozed from the wounds and spurted from severed veins and arteries.

The whole appalling performance was a bestial blood bath. Even the toughest onlookers in the crowd must have blanched at the bedlam.

In spite of a thousand petitions; in spite of awful suffering and self-flagellation; in spite of the frenzy and fury of the false prophets not a single syllable came from their gods. Both Baal and Ashteroth had no word, no answer, no response to their plight.

Even the most cynical and obdurate of the onlookers must have begun to wonder about the veracity of these pagan deities. How could so many prophets be so easily beguiled? Even more astonishing, how could almost a whole nation be so readily deluded? Perhaps for the first time in more than three and a half years a bit of light began to break through the dreadful darkness of spiritual gloom that had engulfed the nation of Israel.

No doubt a substantial percentage of the people massed on Mount Carmel that divine day realized that they had been deceived and double-crossed by the false gods. They had been completely duped because they had taken seriously the smooth, slick insinuations of their deceivers.

It is very much the same in our own late twentieth century. Especially in the church, and among God's people, the time has come when we should take seriously only what God himself reveals and declares to us as truth in his own Word.

Our Western world has pandered to and pursued the false gods of this world far too long. They simply do not have answers to the human dilemma.

13

Elijah Repairs and Prepares the Altar

It had been a long day of dramatic display. The screams, cries, shouts and pleading prayers of the 450 false prophets of Baal had produced no fire. Their wild and fearsome pleadings had not ignited the inert pile of wood laid beneath their butchered bullock. Even the cutting and wounding of their own bodies, the commingling of their own blood and gore with that of the butchered beast, had done nothing but entertain the onlookers. It had all been a pathetic performance—exciting, but empty.

Now the sun was sinking slowly into the western waters of the shining sea. It cast long shadows behind every tree, man and rock on Mount Carmel. The evening hour of the evening sacrifice was approaching. Elijah felt the false prophets had had their fair turn and first fair chance to demonstrate the divinity of their god. Baal had been deaf to their cries, dead to their prayers.

So Elijah, the powerful prophet, standing alone on the summit of Carmel, gestured to the crowd to come near. The hour of truth had come. *"Come near, O Israel!"* he shouted to them through cupped hands. *"Come near to watch what God will do!"*

Skeptical and cynical as most of them were, they gathered around the grizzled desert firebrand. He flung off his mantle, and with heaving muscles and straining back pulled twelve big rough rocks from the mountain soil. These he laid up in three tiers of boulders, four stones to each level. The twelve uncut, unhewn, unshaped, untooled boulders represented the twelve tribes of Israel.

No such altar had been erected in all of Israel for years. No sacrifice of atonement for sin had been made by this stiff-necked people since the gods of Baal and Ashteroth dominated the life of this perverse and polluted people.

But this uncut, rough-laid altar on Mount Carmel also stood as a symbol, a monument, to another great rock altar, uncarved by human hands. It lay nearly a thousand years away in the future—Golgotha (the rock of the skull)—Mount Calvary.

Every rough-laid altar erected by the bare hands of the Hebrew people, without benefit of hammers or chisels, stood as a solemn foreshadowing of that day when God, very God, in the person of his own Son, would offer himself as the supreme sacrifice at Calvary for all men of all time.

Elijah carefully arranged the rough rocks, one upon the other, ready to receive the sacrificial flesh of the bullock. He cried out to Jehovah to justify himself in the presence of this obdurate nation. Let God make bare his great arm, able to save them from their sins. Let him send the fire of his judgment to consume the wood and flesh upon it. Let Jehovah's presence be known, seen and revered among this wayward, willful people. Let his great name be honored again.

It was in the name and authority of God that Elijah

erected the altar. It was the power and prestige of Jehovah that was to be demonstrated on this divine day. Elijah did not come in the name of Elijah. He did not act on his own authority. He stood on Carmel alone, unafraid, defiant, in great dignity, as God's man for this moment.

Upon this rough altar, as of old, and as down through the centuries of human history yet to be unfolded, God would meet man at an altar. The altar stood as the spot where the judgment and mercy of God fell in fire upon sin to consume and cleanse it away. But the altar stood also, and equally, as the spot where the mercy of God fell in love upon man the sinner, now exonerated by the innocent sacrifice offered in his stead and for his salvation.

Around the altar Elijah dug a deep trench, the width of two plow furrows and about as deep. It would separate the place of sacrifice from its surroundings, for this was indeed a unique and sacred spot. It would also hold the equivalent of twelve small casks of water, as well as the hide, entrails, dung and residue left from the butchered bullock. All of this debris, it was always decreed, should also be consumed with the sacrificial fire (read Lev. 4).

It was to be a total sin offering. In its complete consumption by fire, there was depicted the total and complete suffering of our Savior—adequate and sufficient to provide for the full pardon of any penitent.

Elijah went into the surrounding woods that grew so well on Carmel and gathered up great armfuls of dry wood to lay on the altar. Some of the trees had been killed by the long drought. Their limbs and branches had turned bare and brittle. Bleached white by the ruthless, searing sun, they looked like white bones heaped high upon the black rocks of the altar.

Those dead, bare tree limbs spoke eloquently of the "tree," the "cross," the cruel Roman gibbet upon which, 940 years later, God in Christ would himself be laid, as the supreme sacrifice for the sins of all men of all time. This preparation of the altar was an act of enormous significance. It transcended time. It was a prophetic preview of the action Jehovah himself would take to deal with the transgressions of the human race.

Still calling upon the name of the Lord, Elijah then proceeded to butcher the bullock. In careful compliance with Hebrew tradition it was bled carefully. Then quartered and jointed, the pieces were laid upon the dry wood. In the death of this innocent ox, in the spilling of its life-blood there was symbolized the laying down of God's own life. Here there was seen the outpouring of Christ's own spirit and soul and bodily life in substitution for our own. He who was innocent, who knew no sin, being made sin for us that we might be made right with God, with others, with ourselves.

This was the whole basis of redemption, of reconciliation, of restoration for a reprobate person and people. This was the essence of atonement, of forgiveness, of making God and man one—through the substitutionary sacrifice of another.

Then Elijah did a very significant thing. He turned to the watching, murmuring, expectant crowd. His part in the repair and preparation of the altar and sacrifice were over—now it was their turn to participate.

"Fill four barrels with water and pour it over the sacrifice!" It seemed a strange order. Where would they find so much water on such short notice in such dire drought conditions? Springs, streams and fresh water sources were dried up.

But the sea was nearby, just at the foot of Mount Carmel. Its restless waves beat out their eternal rhythm on its beaches. The barrels of water poured upon the sacrifice and altar three times over were pungent, purifying salt water. Twelve barrelfuls in all—a casketful for each of the twelve tribes of this derelict nation.

The significance of the sea water was not lost on Elijah's audience. The ancient edict of Jehovah had ever stood that no sacrifice should ever be offered to him without salt. Salt was absolutely an essential ingredient of every offering.

Salt in the Hebrew tradition and Hebrew culture was a condiment of enormous importance. In fact in very early times salt was considered more precious than gold. In some countries salt was the medium of exchange rather than money.

Salt was essential to life itself. Without salt the body languished.

Salt was the key to strength and stamina in hot countries.

Salt was the common preservative that prevented decay and corruption.

Salt was the condiment that spiced the drab diet of the common people.

Salt was the essential element required for the well-being of livestock.

Salt was the universal medication for healing wounds and sterilizing sores.

Salt was the symbol of friendship and fidelity when shared with another.

Salt stood for the suffering involved in any sacrifice.

This common element of the common man, when added and applied to his humble, simple sacrifice, identified him with his own offering. It was an indication that he, too, was offering himself in penitence to his God. He was being a partaker of the suffering inherent in the sacrifice.

This is why Elijah asked the people to pour the salt-water over the flesh, over the wood, over the rocks of the altar, over the offal, over the whole. In so doing they were enacting the gracious, generous gesture of

God, who, in his sufferings on our behalf, took us with him to Calvary, to cleanse, purify, restore, redeem and reconcile us to himself (read Romans 6 carefully to grasp this).

It was the salt added to the sacrifice which made it a sweet savor. Flesh burned and scorched in the flames alone gives off a disagreeable odor. But when covered and coated in salt, it emits an exquisite fragrance.

Any sacrifice offered apart from and destitute of salt simply was not satisfactory. The donor of the offering had to see it as a substitute for himself. He had to recognize that unless the offering was acceptable to God it had no merit. Its merit lay in the essential concept that the sacrifice bore not only the life of the innocent substitute in one's stead, but also bore the salt therein as a symbol of one's own self being offered up to God. Both ingredients were absolutely essential to its acceptance with God.

When Elijah enjoined all of Israel to pour the twelve barrels of saltwater over the sacrifice, he was providing this perverse and polluted people with a unique opportunity to be identified with himself and his God in offering a satisfactory sacrifice to the Most High. In so many words they were saying, "*We have sinned. We too wish to be identified with this offering. We offer ourselves in contrition and in true penitence of heart. Let your fire of both judgment and mercy fall. May we see your righteousness and your love in the consuming conflagration!*"

From such a heart attitude and such a sacrifice God never does withhold himself. He does hear. He does draw near!

14

Fire Falls

The preparation of the evening sacrifice was complete. Drenched with water, the flesh, wood, stones and soil sparkled in the late evening light. A million sequins of salt glinted in the glow of the setting sun now sinking into the distant horizon of the Mediterranean sea. A path of gold stretched across the sea from the orb of fire to the summit of Mount Carmel.

It was that exquisite hour of breathless stillness which so often settles over the earth at close of day. The heat and glare are gone. The fret and fury of life's delirious pace are eased. The sunset colors tint the sky. And even the most toughened, hardened heart pauses pensively before darkness descends.

Elijah, his rugged features cast in bronze by the golden light, drew near the altar of sacrifice. Not even a single fly buzzed about it. All insect life had been repelled by the saline sea water. The powerful prophet raised his strong, sinewy, sunburned arms toward heaven. He lifted his blazing eyes in burning expectation. His face glowed with hope and heaven's glory. His great voice boomed out like a trumpet blast boldly proclaiming the hour of battle.

"O God, Lord of Abraham, Isaac and Israel, let it be known this day that you, and you alone are God in Israel."

Elijah paused a second or two.

"O God, let it be known I am your servant."

Again he paused momentarily, his hands still uplifted.

"O Jehovah, let it be shown that everything I have done has been at your command."

In his mind's eye Elijah recalled and reviewed in a few split seconds all the momentous events of the past 42 months. His foretelling the famine; the desperate days at Cherith; the years in the widow's house; the raising of her son; his return to public view.

Elijah recalled his encounter with the king's chamberlain Obadiah; his second challenge to the wicked Ahab; the dreadful drama of this long hot day with the prophets of Baal in their frustrated frenzy; his own careful, meticulous, painstaking preparation of the evening sacrifice.

Yes, indeed! Everything he had done; every step he had taken; every move he had made; every word he had spoken had been ordered and directed by God. He was a man under command. He was a soul submissive to the sovereign Spirit of God, a person promptly obedient to the will and wish of the Most High. No wonder he was a prophet of such power.

Just as the whole of the sacrifice, the wood, the altar, the soil upon which he now stood had been soaked, saturated and literally submerged in water, so his own soul, spirit and body had been submerged and saturated and soaked in the Word of the Lord. All was within the will of Jehovah God.

With enormous assurance Elijah, a man right with God, right with others, right with himself cried out now in flaming faith and ringing confidence.

"Hear me, O Lord God, hear me! Respond in

positive proof that this perverse, petulant people may know assuredly that you are God very God, calling them back in repentance: turning them to yourself once more!"

This was his prayer of faith.

This was a petition that could not be denied.

This was a heart cry that God would hear and honor.

A flash of fierce celestial fire fell upon the evening sacrifice. The flames blazed and burned with fury. The temperatures were so intense the water was instantly turned to steam. The great joints of beef and piles of wet wood were consumed in moments. Even the twelve large boulders and the damp soil all around were oxidized and obliterated by the holocaust.

It was all over in a few short seconds.

Like a lightning bolt the fire did its deadly work instantaneously. Where moments before an altar and sacrifice had stood shining in the sun, there now remained only a burned, fire-blackened depression in the scorched soil. God's presence, power and person had taken and consumed everything offered.

Elijah, alone, stood still on the summit of Carmel. He alone was not flat on his face. He alone was unmoved, unafraid, undisturbed. He was a man who kept company with God. What he had requested he had received. Jehovah was his friend. Again God had shown himself faithful to his servant.

But all around him, thousands and thousands of his countrymen were flat on their faces. Too frightened to look up—too frightened to raise their eyes lest they too be consumed with fire. Too alarmed to face the God whom they had spurned, they cried out in unison.

"The Lord Jehovah, he is the God! The Lord Jehovah, he alone is the God!"

It is significant that they did not exclaim: *"The Lord he is* OUR *God!"*

This incredible and remarkable display of God's

presence had the effect of bringing the people of Israel back to their beginnings. When God had declared himself to Abraham, the founder of their race, he had confirmed his covenant by coming down in a flame to consume Abraham's evening sacrifice (read Genesis 15).

In a similar manner when Jehovah delivered the nation of Israel out of Egypt he made his presence real to them in the cloud by day and the pillar of fire by night.

When in the fullness of time the great ordinances of God were given to Israel for their conduct as his chosen people, the fire from heaven descended upon Mount Sinai in great power and presence.

Over and over fire was used in subsequent visitations to reveal to Israel that the presence of their God was not just empty superstition.

In the power and potency of that divine presence, Elijah now called out triumphantly to the prostrate crowd. *"Seize the false prophets of Baal. Don't let a single one escape!"*

Too long these imposters had ensnared and enslaved the nation of Israel. Too long they had imposed their wicked ways on Israel. Too long they had led them down into debauchery and disgusting degradation. Their hour of judgment had come.

Just as the fire of judgment had consumed the whole sacrifice on the altar, so now the awesome judgment of a righteous God would fall upon these counterfeit prophets who pretended to speak for God.

The captives were led down to the now dry stream bed of the brook Kishon. Appropriately enough its modern name means "the ensnarer." There in that dry donga those who had ensnared Israel would be put to death. The end had come for the influence of Baal in the land.

Too often the children of Israel had turned to this

false god and his false prophets for support and succor. Always they had been betrayed and deceived. In their folly and blindness Israel had followed the false gods of their pagan neighbors. Elijah now was determined the deception should end.

In righteous anger and blazing indignation the fiery prophet commanded the people to help him exterminate this evil scourge that had enslaved them for so long.

We are not given the grim and gory details of how the 450 false prophets of Baal were put to death. We know only that it was done.

It stands as a solemn reminder to us that men cannot go on sinning with impunity and not face an ultimate hour of drastic retribution. God is a God of love, compassion, concern and incredible patience. He calls to all men to turn to him and live. But those who willfully, deliberately, stubbornly spurn his overtures of compassion, ultimately decide their own destination. It is their will not his that brings death.

But over and beyond this there lies an enormous lesson for God's own people. Only God himself could send down celestial fire on Carmel. Only his presence and power could be so potent as to completely consume all of the altar and its sacrifice. Only in this way could all of Israel be convinced of his care, concern and compassion for them as a people.

Having seen this demonstration of his enormous integrity and fidelity to both them and himself, they now in turn had the serious obligation of seizing the false prophets. They had come to grips with the false gods, those who for too long had ensnared their loyalties and devotion.

This simply had to happen before there could come rain again to refresh their land and revive their own lives. The last vestiges and falsehoods of the old life style had to be brought to an end.

Precisely the same divine principle applies to us today. If a man or woman sees clearly what God has accomplished at Calvary, of which Carmel was a foreshadowing, then there are certain positive steps of genuine repentance which must be taken.

At Calvary, on the cross, the fierce judgment for our sins fell upon Christ. There he bore and absorbed the penalty for our wrongdoings, for our pride, for our pollution, for our perverseness. There, too, were demonstrated the divine caring and concern of our Heavenly Father. There his integrity, his fidelity and his faithfulness were displayed in bounteous generosity.

Out of gratitude those of us who even feebly understand his compassion will, in turn, tear away the false gods and falsehoods from our lives. There will sweep into our spirits and souls the unshakable conviction that we for our part must do away with the duplicity, the deception, the devilment which have so long dogged us. We must be done with them. This is true repentance. This is genuine conversion. This is sincere conviction in the believer and in the church.

And it always precedes the sound of the approaching rain of revival.

15

Rain Returns

The massacre of Baal's false prophets down at the dried-up donga of the brook Kishon was an event of horrendous magnitude for Israel. Yet not for Israel alone, but also for her monarch—Ahab—and for her prophet Elijah. All their lives thereafter would never be quite the same again.

The death of the deceivers marked the close of a scandalous chapter in the tragic tale of this tempestuous people. It marked the end of the fearful famine that had ruined the land. It was the last page in the sad story of a nation almost wholly separated from its God, Jehovah.

It was down in the desolate, blood-stained, bone-dry streambed of this desperate donga that Elijah detected the distant sound of approaching rain. The skies overhead were still hot, brittle, blue, pulsing with heat. The land all around still panted with burning temperatures. Not a cloud, even one as small as an olive leaf, hovered on the horizon.

Yet rain was in the offing!

A wind was blowing up!

There was the sound of an approaching rainstorm!

Perhaps others could not detect it on the wind.

But the powerful prophet of God could!

He was attuned and sensitive to the movement of God's Spirit both in the wind off the sea and the wind that was at work in his own spirit.

The fierce desert firebrand, his being ablaze with the power and presence of God who had just granted him such a colossal conquest over Baal, turned to the weary Ahab: *"Refresh yourself, O King, eat and drink."*

As for Elijah, he had other work to do. He had another appointment with God, back up on the crest of Carmel. He had meat and drink of which Ahab knew nothing. He drew his strength from the LORD, not from his surroundings.

Ahab proceeded to prepare himself a banquet, while Elijah proceeded to a private place of prayer. He and he alone would now prevail upon Jehovah to revive the land with refreshing rain.

It is appropriate to pause at this point and reflect upon what was really happening at this historic moment. First of all, we simply must see that before there could be any blessing from above, there had to be a brokenness before the Lord. Not only had the famine devastated Israel, but so also had the fire that fell on Carmel compelled them to fall on their faces in total obeisance to the power and presence of God. Now here at Kishon the last vestige of their dependence on false prophets and false gods had been obliterated.

In other words, Israel stood stripped of every means of either physical or spiritual support. This was a people bowed and broken before their God. They were humbled in heart, prostrate in spirit.

Before there can come blessing there must be brokenness.

Before there can be refreshing there must be repentance.

Before there can be new life, the old must be put to death.

These are the essential, basic principles which never change, and upon which God's promises to his people are predicated.

Almost one hundred years before this dreadful day on Carmel, King Solomon had stood before all of Israel in the presence of God. In his majestic prayer of dedication for the magnificent and glorious temple built for the glory of God, he had requested the presence and power of Jehovah to fill that glorious edifice. He had entreated the Lord to listen to the pleas of his people amid all their perverseness and pride.

In response the Word of God given to him in bold and unshakable assurance was:

> And the Lord appeared to Solomon by night, and said unto him, I have heard thy prayer, and have chosen this place to myself for a house of sacrifice. If I shut up heaven that there be no rain, or if I command the locusts to devour the land, or if I send pestilence among my people;
>
> If my people, which are called by my name, shall humble themselves, and pray, and seek my face, and turn from their wicked ways; then will I hear from heaven, and will forgive their sin, and will heal their land. Now mine eyes shall be open and mine ears attent unto the prayer that is made in this place (2 Chron. 7:12–15).

Elijah knew, remembered, and depended upon this divine declaration. Israel was humbled. Israel was repentant. Israel was ready now to be refreshed and revived. God would restore his people.

And it must be added here that the same powerful, potent promises apply to any person or people at any point in time. God delights to draw near to those who are of a broken and contrite spirit. He enjoys bestowing his benefits and blessings upon those who recognize his presence and power. He loves to share his bounty with those who make a clean break with the world's ways, determining to do his will and walk in his way. He ever looks for those who will respond to his overtures and keep company with him.

God had found such a soul in Elijah.

His kind are few and far between.

The solitary soul who seeks his sole support from God is a distinct rarity in society.

It had been a long, long day for Elijah. The great crowds of excited people who had assembled on Carmel had all dispersed. Chattering excitedly about the unbelievable events of this momentous day, they had trailed off home in their trickling lines. The news of the fire from heaven and the ghastly slaughter of the false prophets would spread like wildfire far and wide across the whole of Palestine.

Ahab had gone back to his banqueting.

For everyone but Elijah it was pretty much "business as usual."

Alone now except for his servant boy, the son of the widow from Zarephath, the boy whom he had raised from the dead, Elijah prostrated himself on the summit of Carmel.

Once before he had entreated God in this spot to send down fire from heaven.

Now a second time he would beseech Jehovah to send down rain from heaven.

On the first occasion his prayers had been made in public.

Now on this second occasion they would be in private.

Facing out to sea, his head bowed low between his knees, kneeling prostrate on the dry, dusty soil, Elijah waited upon God to send rain.

The first time he prayed for fire it fell at once.

This time when he asked for rain there was a long wait.

Six times the fiery-eyed prophet sent his young servant lad to scan the western sky for signs of rain. Six times the boy came back with bad news. "*There is nothing.*"

Not even the faintest shred of a cloud crossed the sky. The Mediterranean Sea lay stretched out like an azure-blue blanket beneath a burning blue sky. And though the youth's eager eyes were just as keen to detect the first signs of rain as were Elijah's—nothing came to view. The sky was empty.

But this did not deter Elijah. He was not to be discouraged by the mere appearance of things. Just because his servant boy was discouraged, Elijah's faith in God never faltered.

Again and again and again he was told: "*There is nothing.*" It seemed to be a hopeless situation. There was not a single sign on the horizon of any change in the climate. A lesser man would have given way to doubt. Perhaps he had been too presumptuous in prophesying the rain. Perhaps he would be made to look like a fool if rain did not fall. Had he indulged in excessive self-delusion when he heard the distant sound of a storm?

These and a score of other searing, searching, unsettling questions may have rushed and tumbled in violent turmoil through Elijah's spirit. After all, he was a man of passions similar to our own. He was as susceptible to unsettling misgivings as we are.

But Elijah kept his head bowed between his bended knees. It could be in no better place. At least in that position he could not see the brassy skies, the blazing sun or the unpromising horizon to the west. He was not preoccupied with the circumstantial evidence to the contrary all around him.

Instead, he was a humble man shut up to his God.

He was closed into his closet, a narrow confine betwixt his knees.

He saw God and God alone.

It was in God, and only in God, that Elijah's faith reposed—not in the boy's report. What if the weather did look static? What if the climate did appear contrary? What if the sky did look as barren as brass?

It was not the circumstances that counted.

It was not the boy's estimation of the situation that mattered.

It was not the events of the day that could deter him.

Rain was on its way! God could be counted on to come through! God was bound to be faithful to himself and his servant and his people! God would deliver them from the drought!

So a seventh time Elijah sent his servant lad to scan the sea. Out of the vastness of the waves, strength and succor and sweet rain would come.

And the seventh time the young man spotted a cloud. Was it really a cloud? Or was it water vapor beginning to accumulate that would quickly evaporate? It was a tiny speck on the western horizon. Some translations say it was at first no larger than the size of a man's hand. The quaint and beautiful Knox version states it was the size of a person's footprint.

This I love, for in the book of Nahum we read, *"The Lord hath his way in the whirlwind and in the storm, and the clouds are the dust of his feet"* (Nah. 1:3).

Elijah needed to be told no more. He knew God was on his way, bringing rain. This tiny cloud was the first sure sign that a tremendous storm was on its way.

Without despairing, without faltering in his faith, the powerful prophet had prevailed in prayer until the ultimate completion of his petition was assured. That he did this seven times is more than mere coincidence, for in God's economy seven represents fulfillment, completion and finality.

Elijah had not allowed anything or anyone to deter him. He was a man right with God. He was a man in accord with God's will. He was a man of unshakable confidence in the Lord.

Elijah lifted himself from the dusty ground. He brushed the dry soil from his sunburned knees. His blazing eyes took on a fierce new light as he looked out across the sea. A great storm was brewing. Giant, ominous thunderheads climbed thousands of feet into the sky on huge thermals. A wind began to blow in off the sea.

In exultation he sent his servant scurrying down to Ahab at the foot of Carmel. *"Ready your chariot. Head for home. There's a terrific storm that will soon overtake you!"*

It may have sounded like madness from a raving maniac. But by now Ahab had heard and seen Elijah's predictions fulfilled often enough that he no longer ignored them. He had learned that Elijah was a man in touch with God. And not even a monarch could ignore such an individual. What Elijah said, Ahab did.

If Elijah said a storm was coming up out of the sea, Ahab was by now ready to believe him. In fact it seems Ahab was much more impressed by Elijah the prophet than he was by Elijah's God. He seemed to hold the flaming firebrand in much greater regard than he did Jehovah.

As for Elijah it must be said to his credit that though he abhorred the wicked ways of Ahab, he never actually attacked him in vengeance or acted disrespectfully toward his king. No doubt he recognized that Ahab was the man of God's appointment for this dark hour in Israel's tragic history. His responsibility before God was not to indulge in a personal vendetta against this dreadful monarch, but to fearlessly call his people back to God in spite of all Ahab's despicable deeds.

Elijah had demonstrated again that God was faithful, trustworthy and reliable. Just as this tremendous wind and storm and rain now swept in off the sea again to refresh the land, so the mercies and benefits of God come sweeping to us again from out of the giant seas of his own graciousness, goodness and generosity shown to the children of men. There do come seasons of renewal and revival because God is faithful to his own and to himself.

16

The Hour of Power

For three and a half years there had not been such a storm in Palestine. The sky was black. Huge clouds, heavy with rain, rolled in off the Mediterranean. They were driven by a powerful wind that drove surging whitecaps thundering onto the coastal beaches. The gale rattled the dry leaves on the parched trees. Lightning flashed. It lit the darkened sky from horizon to horizon. Thunder rolled and rumbled across the land. And the first drops of rain in forty-two desperate months splashed down into the dry dust.

The dry, sun-scorched earth could scarcely receive the rain. The soil was baked hard. Here and there the running rivulets gathered in muddy pools. The moisture instead of soaking down into the subsoil sealed the surface, so that water began to cascade off fields and slopes and hills in rushing flood torrents. In just a short time flash floods raged down every stream bed and dry donga, rampaging back down to the sea from whence the rain had come.

Ahab saw and sensed all this. He knew that unless he raced for home in his chariot, his route would soon be cut off and he would be marooned on Mount

Carmel. So he gave his prancing horses full rein and headed home for Jezreel, some twenty miles away.

The horses ran like the wind that blew in off the sea. The fresh aroma of falling rain filled their nostrils and stirred their blood. The electric excitement of lightning flashes and crashing thunder stirred their spirits. They took the bits hard in their teeth and began to gallop. They needed no urging, for they were headed for home, their spacious palace stables. Nothing could stop them. Manes flying, hooves churning up the dust, now turning to mud, they raced wildly across the country. Ahab clung to the reins as his chariot rattled noisily beneath his feet.

But the king was not travelling alone. He looked back momentarily to see if the storm clouds were overtaking him. What he saw, instead, awed and frightened him. It was the figure of the fiery Elijah racing up beside him. Fierce as a desert falcon, fleet as a desert gazelle, the powerful prophet sped alongside Ahab with a burst of rushing speed.

In just a few short seconds the bearded firebrand, his tough, lean figure moving with majestic, muscular power had passed the startled chariot horses. Now he ran ahead of them. Each stride he took was like the long easy lope of an antelope on the run. With apparent ease the prophet outpaced the king's chariot. He was running freely just in front of the horses that plunged ahead wildly, racing to keep up with him.

The best of cross-country runners may have been able to maintain this furious pace for five or six miles. Elijah did it for twenty. His body was bare. Only a brief loincloth, cinched tight with a well-worn leather belt, was wrapped around his waist. He ran free as the wind that blew the dry leaves and dust about him. He ran with powerful thrusts of his limbs that shone damp with perspiration under the darkening skies. Sporadic flashes of lightning lit up his rugged face, wreathed in a smile of tremendous vitality.

The hand of God was upon Elijah. This was his hour of power. He felt a surge of vigor flowing through his veins such as he had never known before. The Spirit of God empowered him with a strength and stamina that surpassed anything he had ever sensed before.

For Elijah this was his moment of glory. Behind him were the dread days of Cherith, Zarephath, Carmel and Kishon. He was a spirit set free. Superb in all his splendor as a man—God's man—he outran Ahab's chariot and raced full speed through the city gates into Jezreel.

The prophet had reached his pinnacle of power!

But he also had reached a point of great peril.

His majestic marathon had been a moment of glory.

But, as with the best of men, it was also a wrong and dangerous move.

There is absolutely nothing to indicate in the scriptural record that it was God who sent him to Jezreel. There is no mention made that as with every other previous step he had taken, this action was in direct response to the revealed word of the Lord.

It is true we are told that the hand of God was upon this man in a significant way. But the Lord's intentions for Elijah were not necessarily that he should display himself with such bravado. One wonders if it was in keeping with his previous pattern of behavior before the Lord to act so blatantly in a show of personal prowess.

Elijah was a man with passions like the rest of us. He was not beyond being proud and lifted up by the series of enormous successes he had seen under God's good hand. Perhaps now for the first time in his meteoric career he had taken the bit between his own teeth and was heading in a direction of his own choosing. Perhaps for the first time this "righteous man" was resorting to his own schemes, indulging his own desires, doing his own thing.

Outdistancing the king's chariot was a tremendous

feat of endurance. Outrunning his monarch's swift Arabian horses, finest in the world, was an achievement no other man could ever match, perhaps even in our twentieth-century Olympics. Outpacing all his contemporaries may have seemed to Elijah like the finest culmination of his career. What greater accolade could a man hope to achieve? And above all he had brought rain!

Surely now he would be given the public recognition he deserved. Surely now he would no longer have to be a prophet in hiding, living furtively underground in places like Cherith and Zarephath. Surely now he might even be wined and dined at the royal table in Jezreel. After all Ahab was impressed.

Such times and such temptations come to the very best of God's servants and saints. Few, very few indeed, are the men and women who can endure fame or taste the heady wine of power without enormous peril.

Prosperity, prestige, prominence, even in the service of the Lord, have an insidious capacity to pervert and corrupt the choicest characters. The inherent pride of the human spirit is so sinister that it is ever ready to reassert itself with the least provocation.

Individuals who may have remained unknown, unsung, unrecognized for years, when abruptly thrust into the fierce exposure of the stage lights, may stumble and fall. Few are the people who seem able to handle success very well. The simplicity of their early beginnings, the austerity of their humble walk with God are too often swiftly eclipsed by the rising sun of their own sudden popularity and prominence. In the heat and fervor of their glory they often forget the God who has given them great success.

For Elijah to leave the sublime, solitary summit of Carmel and go down into the sordidness of Jezreel, where Jezebel still held sway, was like Lot, that other "righteous man" who left the hills of Abraham and pitched his tent toward Sodom and Gomorrah. There is a profound parallel between the performances of these two select and special souls.

When Lot looked out across the fertile plains of the Jordan he was fascinated by what he saw. It drew him. It enticed him. Finally it was in that easy place that he nearly perished. It was there he lost his fame, his fortune and his family. It was to be the low point of his whole life before the Lord.

Similarly, when Elijah chose to go down to the royal capital city of Jezreel instead of staying alone with God on Carmel, he was placing himself in dreadful jeopardy. Jezreel was Jezebel's bizarre stronghold. Jezreel was where the power of Ashteroth still prevailed. Jezreel was where Israel had first encountered the iron chariots of the Canaanites. Jezreel was where others of Elijah's predecessors had fallen before the enemy. Jezreel was where Elijah would descend from triumph to tragedy.

17

Elijah in Despair

When Ahab returned to his palace at Jezreel he was literally bursting with exciting news. He had left a few days before to look for grass and pasturage for his horses. Now he came back with rain pouring from the clouds overhead. He bore, too, the awesome report of events on Carmel and down at Kishon.

It was not the sort of thing that would cheer his malevolent queen. During Elijah's long absence from public view this vicious, wicked woman had pretty much had her own way in Israel. Even though she was not an Israeli, but a foreign Sidonian, she had used her position and influence as queen to dominate not only her weak-kneed husband, but also this spineless nation.

Jezebel had usurped the rightful authority of her husband. She had put to death all the prophets of Jehovah, despite her chamberlain's attempt to rescue a hundred of them. She had stifled the true spiritual life of the nation. She had brought in a multitude of false prophets to perform the licentious rites of Baal and Ashteroth. Literally she wallowed in the moral revolution she had perpetrated. She gloated over the sexual orgies and perverted prostitution that had corrupted Israel like cancer consuming its society from within its vitals.

She had succeeded in subverting multitudes.

Then suddenly Ahab came back with the news of what had transpired at Carmel and the brook Kishon. Elijah the powerful prophet of the Most High had suddenly reappeared. First he had confronted Obadiah, the lord chamberlain. Then he had challenged Ahab himself. Then he had called all Israel to Carmel. Obviously Elijah was invincible. He was a giant who had stepped back on center stage in the life of Israel. It was he who had called down fire from heaven. It was he who urged the crowds to capture all the prophets of Baal. It was he who had put them to death. It was Elijah who called down rain from the skies. It was he who outran Ahab's chariot to Jezreel. Elijah could not be stopped!

Instead of being intimidated, Jezebel was infuriated. She flew into a fearsome rage.

Who would stop whom?

She herself would put a full stop to Elijah's exploits. She herself would end his influence in Israel. She herself would see to it that this flaming desert firebrand was quenched quickly. She would have him murdered within twenty-four hours.

It was the inevitable story of the eternal conflict between good and evil that rages relentlessly upon earth. It is surprising how few, even within the church, are acutely aware of this battle that is fought unceasingly.

Evil cannot tolerate righteousness.

Darkness is opposed to light.

Death attempts to destroy life.

Hatred is set against love.

Deception is determined to obliterate truth.

The fierce contest between right and wrong never

relents. And Jezebel was determined her evil devices would win the day. In her blind folly and arrogant ignorance she was sure that she was only murdering a man. What she could not see in her spiritual degradation was that she had literally set herself against God. Ultimately this would be her own total undoing, for in the end good does overcome evil. Light does dispel darkness. Life triumphs over death. Love conquers hatred. And in the end God always has the last word.

As the people of God it is essential that we see this.

In these closing decades of the twentieth century, we see fierce foes of God's people determined to destroy them. National and international forces are at work in the world endeavoring to demolish the church and quench God's voice. They will do everything possible to put an end to truth.

Though temporarily they may appear to succeed, in the end it is God who will triumph. It is he who shall have the final word as to the destiny of men and nations.

We do well to remind ourselves of this when events look so dark.

Elijah should have done this, but somehow and for some obscure reason he did not.

Instead, when word was brought to him that Jezebel was set on his slaughter, he suddenly succumbed to her evil intent and saw only his own peril. Her threat to his life suddenly sent Elijah into a black funk of despair. All he could think of was to escape her cruel clutches.

It was one of the most traumatic and tragic "turnarounds" ever recorded of a great and godly man of God.

One can only conjecture that the rising crescendo of heady events that led up to this point must have gone to the powerful prophet's head a bit. Perhaps in an unguarded show of pride he had strutted around the streets of Jezreel in full view. After all, everyone knew now who he was! No longer was he the recluse from the desert wastes. No longer was he the obscure, unsung prophet who was a rather hazy legend with his people. Now he was the notorious, yet unknown firebrand of God who at will could call for either fire or water from heaven!

Here he was in flesh and blood and bones out in plain view for all the people to see. He was where Jezebel could see him until her blood boiled with rage. He was out in the open where she could get at him. He was her public enemy number one, an easy target for her tantrums. He had fallen prey to pride, and now he was in enormous peril.

Pride has its own insidious way of undoing the best of people. It can lay a giant in the dust of despair in the wink of an eye. It can land any hero in the ditch of despondency in less time than it takes me to pen these words.

Pride leads a person to become so self-preoccupied that all his interest, all his attention, all his energy is focused exclusively on himself and his own preservation.

This was Elijah's position at this point of peril.

Only one thing did he see: *"The threat to himself."*

So preoccupied had he become with his own survival no longer could he see either God, or God's hand upon him.

And so he fled.

He would not face Jezebel.

He was overwhelmed and engulfed with fear and foreboding.

Like a hunted hare, he took his servant lad and departed the city, running hard, headed south for the desert wastes beyond Beersheba.

Elijah's faith in God was gone.

Elijah's confidence that right would win was shattered.

Elijah's assurance that Jehovah was God, was now shaken.

The focus of his attention was no longer on what God could do, but on what he, Elijah, the cunning, skilled, desert nomad could do—to save himself.

Elijah was falling back on his own survival skills, his own desert expertise, his own outdoor experience. He had allowed the threat from Jezebel to intrude itself between him and his Lord. The circumstances of his crisis had come between him and his God. He saw now only his own peril, not the possibilities or potential power in the hand of God on his person.

We all do this at times. Often in sudden, unexpected crises, our eyes are diverted from the power and presence of Christ, to the threatening circle of circumstances closing in around us. Our faith fails and we want to run for our lives.

Happily enough for Elijah, he was man enough not to take his servant lad with him down into the desert of his own desperate despondency. Instead he instructed the boy to stay in Beersheba. He himself would go on alone to face ultimate humiliation in solitude. Elijah obviously did not want the lad to share in his personal failure or to be shaken in his own frail faith.

It was bad enough for Elijah to have turned tail and fled in the face of a woman's fury. But it would be the worst sort of calumny for the lad to see his hero lose all faith in Jehovah God because of it. That would never, never do!

Elijah was determined to put as much distance as possible between himself and Jezebel's "hit-men." If he could outpace Ahab's chariot, he could also outrun the queen's henchmen. Even if the murderers rode fast chariots they could not catch this fleet-footed desert gazelle. So he sped on south, deep into the desolate wastes of the Negev desert.

This was not God's arrangement for Elijah. It was his own idea. As Knox's translation puts it so pungently for us: *"Elijah took fright and set out upon a journey of his own devising"* (2 Kings 19:3).

For a whole day Elijah fled, running with bated breath and heaving chest; running until his lungs would nearly burst; running till his mouth grew parched with inhaling the dry desert air; running until his powerful legs would carry him no longer. At last he saw a scrubby juniper tree, not much larger than a big broom bush. He stumbled toward it and collapsed in its scraggly shade.

He knew, as a desert nomad, that a man, in utter extremity, could at least survive on the stringy roots of this scrubby desert tree. There was sufficient moisture and nourishment in juniper roots to keep death at bay for a day or two (read Job 30:1–4).

But at this low point in his career, Elijah wasn't even sure he wanted to survive. In his despondency and despair of divided emotions he thought it might even be better to die. After all why carry on at all? What good had it done for him to defy all the forces of evil at work in this world? He had seemed to change nothing. He had accomplished no more than his forefathers in the fight for right. Wickedness was still in the place of power. Sin still held sway. Why not just ask God to carry him away? It was all over! He had had enough!

Even great men, yes, the best of men feel beaten and beleaguered at times. They are down in the ditch of despair.

In this state of utter despondency and dismay Elijah, utterly exhausted by his own exercise in self-preservation, fell sound asleep.

He had completely forgotten that God's presence was with him under the juniper as much as it had been on Carmel.

18

Awakened by an Angel

Amid his despair and despondency Elijah had obviously forgotten the faithfulness of God to him. Somehow there had vanished from his view all the amazing achievements and exciting experiences of his years of service to Jehovah. It was an impressive list that should have burned white hot in his remembrance:

The famine he foretold came to pass.

He had been fed by ravens.

The widow's barrel of flour and jar of oil never ran dry.

He had seen the woman's son raised to life.

There had been the celestial fire from God on Carmel.

The rains had returned again at his request.

With supernatural stamina he had outraced the king's chariot.

These were seven remarkable demonstrations to a skeptical society that his God was very much alive, active, at work in the affairs of individuals and nations. Yet even with all this evidence in hand Elijah was totally depressed. He was in a miserable mood of melancholy. He didn't care if he did die. In fact he asked God to take his life from him.

In this state he fell fast asleep in the sparse shade of the little struggling juniper tree.

Elijah did not realize that he himself had been as great a source of shade and solace to all of Israel during their dreadful drought, both physical and spiritual, as the juniper bush was to him.

What if the juniper had shriveled up and died in the desert?

What if he were to be removed from the stage of Israel's public life at this point? No, indeed, if a solitary juniper tree had no more purpose for its life than to supply shade for one solitary man struggling in the desert of despair its life was worthwhile. And for Elijah there was still significant work to do under God's great hand, even if it was only to be his voice in the desert calling Israel back to himself.

Most of us have our "desert days" of despair. There are times when we forget the faithfulness of our Lord. God seems to become remote and far removed from our struggles. Life seems a relentless, remorseless erosion of our stamina and strength in the struggle to carry on. There seems to be much more pain than pleasure in the pattern of our days. Forgetting the unremitting faithfulness of God to us in the past, we focus only on the futility and frustrations of the present. We can see no hope or cheering prospect for the future.

What we need, and need desperately at this low point, is a new touch upon us from God himself.

Christ's Gracious Spirit, our constant companion, must again reassure us of his willingness to sustain, encourage and refresh us.

This the Lord did for Elijah.

For the angel which touched the dear man was none other than the person of God himself in disguise.

> In all their affliction he was afflicted, and the Angel of his presence saved them: in his love and in his pity he redeemed them; and he bare them, and carried them all the days of old (Isa. 63:9).

His word to Elijah was simple, direct, potent. "*Arise! Eat!*" The famished prophet needed food, drink and rest. He needed restoration from fatigue. He needed rebuilding after the fierce fray of the previous days. It is no simple thing to be called of God to challenge the forces of evil singlehandedly in a corrupt culture. The contest had been a triumph, but it had also taken its toll of Elijah's strength.

In his amazing mercy and gracious understanding our Lord always remembers that we are made from dust. He never forgets that we are shaped from the fragile, fickle fabric of fallible human nature. He deals with us in enormous empathy and insight. He extends endless compassion, comfort and consolation to his earth children drawn from the fragile family of man.

God did not rebuke Elijah. He did not reproach him for his despair, nor did he recriminate with him for forgetting his faithfulness. Instead God touched, restored and revitalized Elijah.

When Elijah stirred himself, shook the sleep from his eyes and looked up, there was a *japate* toasting on a bed of hot coals. Beside it stood a cruse of clear cool water. It was a precise preview of the dawn breakfast Jesus prepared for his discouraged disciples on the beach of Lake Galilee nearly 950 years later. They too had been discouraged and dismayed by the events of their time, when Christ came to touch them at the point of their extremity.

Utterly exhausted, Elijah fell fast asleep again after eating the delicious fresh baked bread and draining the cruse of refreshing water.

A second time the angel awakened him. He was

again urged to eat and drink heartily for there was a tremendous trip ahead of him. Unknown to the powerful prophet, what had started out as a mere scramble to survive was to terminate in a most remarkable encounter with God in the solitude of Sinai.

When Elijah headed south into the Negev to elude Jezebel's killers, he had no idea his flight would take him hundreds of miles across some of the most desolate desperate desert wasteland in all the world. The winding route he would have to follow threaded its way amid the dry dongas, fierce mountains and burning sands of the Sinai peninsula. It was at least 300 miles of torture under terrifying temperatures.

Even the best of camel caravans, laden with ample food, supplies of water and tents to shelter from the burning sun, took weeks to cross this terrible terrain. Elijah would be on the way for forty days and forty nights. All he had to shelter him from the formidable elements was his mantle, loincloth, stout sandals, and supernatural stamina from Jehovah.

Like a hound, headed for home, across impossible barriers, nothing would deter the fierce desert firebrand till he set foot on the slopes of Sinai.

For forty dreadful days and forty lonely nights, almost six solid weeks, Elijah heard only the dry desert wind in the wadis by day and the raucous cries of the ravens and the yapping of jackals or howl of hyenas by night. He was alone, very much alone, going over some of the same grim ground through which God had led Israel for forty years in her wretched wilderness wanderings.

He was going back to the beginnings of his people. He was going back to the same spiritual mount from which God had spoken to Moses in smoke and flames and dark clouds. He was going back to the very same cave, the cleft in the selfsame rock where God had hidden Moses when he passed by to show his servant his own great glory.

Elijah was drawn on, irresistibly southward toward the same secluded, solitary, sublime spot where Moses had himself fasted twice for forty days and forty nights. It was during the purification of this dire ordeal of self-cleansing and self-purging that men's souls were stripped of sensual desire. Thus their spirits asserted preeminent place in still communion with the infinite Spirit of the Most High.

Here under the pulsing desert stars, in the intense stillness of the desert's solitude, Elijah again would hear the clear, unmistakable voice of the Almighty. Again he would hear from heaven. He would be instructed clearly as to his next commission.

On Sinai there would be no conflicting voices to confuse him. He would be free from the accolades of the crowds who had seen his great conquest on Carmel. He would be exempt from the duplicity of the devilish Ahab. He would be clear of the terrible threats of Jezebel. Not even the kind and thoughtful solicitudes of his gentle servant lad were there to sway his feelings or turn his thoughts.

Elijah was alone with his God.

Elijah was in the place of God's appointment.

Elijah really was back at the initial base of his own beginnings. He needed again to hear a word from God.

There is a tremendous truth here that we all should see. As God's people we cannot hope to be sustained in our service for the Lord by the stimulus of past experiences. No matter how startling the exploits experienced—no matter how great the former faithfulness to God—we cannot serve in the strength of past performances.

I do not live today on the energy of last week's food. Each new morning, I must find fresh nourishment for this day's work.

I do not run on my reputation. I must run in the sustenance and stamina derived from God today. There has to be a fresh infusion of life from above for each new adventure I engage in with God. I cannot coast along on past conquests. I need a new touch, a fresh filling, supernatural strength from the Lord for this day, during this day.

Christ himself made this very clear. We are to ask daily for our daily bread. *He* is that bread. *He* is our drink. *He* is our energy. *He* is our life. *"The words that I speak unto you, they are spirit, and they are life"* (John 6:63). Here is the daily source, the daily supply of spiritual stamina for service.

This is what Elijah needed and needed desperately. A man in despair, a man destitute in spirit, a man discouraged by the toughness of his times, he had to hear again from God.

Strange as it may seem to us, that word from the Lord came, but it was couched in a peculiar question.

"Elijah—what are you doing here, crouched in this cave?" As if God didn't know. Just as when he asked Adam and Eve their first question when they tried to hide from his presence: "Adam, Eve—where are you?"

Whenever the Lord lays his hand upon us in caring concern—whenever he speaks to us in compassion—he invites us to consider very carefully where we are. Why are we at that particular point in life? It is time to take stock of our situation—time to be utterly still and hear him speak.

19

Elijah on Sinai

Elijah's visit to Mount Sinai was not just an event arranged by him. God's hand was on this man. He was here by divine appointment for a very special purpose, which he himself may not have fully understood at that juncture of his life.

It was no small thing to be shunted back and forth as he had been, first from utter obscurity in Gilead to the very court of Ahab and Jezebel. Then back out into the lonely desert donga of Cherith until it dried up. From there to Zarephath and the widow's home on the doorstep of Ethbaal. Back again to face Ahab and all Israel on Carmel. Then again into Jezreel and the presence of his archenemy Jezebel. Now again out into the desert and down to this stern, remote and forbidding mountain overlooking the Red Sea.

Elijah may have felt a bit like a human yo-yo flung hither and thither, in and out, up and down, back and forth across the forbidding extremities of the Middle East. Apparently he had no permanent home, no place to really call his own, no spot to rest his head. Very much like our Lord during his years of public ministry, he was without a regular residence. He was always on the move, always under orders from the Spirit of God. The strain must have been enormous.

Added to this Elijah bore a heavy burden of deep spiritual concern for the people of Israel. With a deep intuition he sensed that they had set their feet on the final path of their own inevitable destruction. Asked why he was holed up in the obscure cave on Mount Sinai, his immediate reply was: ". . . I have been very jealous for the Lord God of hosts: for the children of Israel have forsaken thy covenant, thrown down thine altars, and slain thy prophets with the sword; and I, even I only, am left; and they seek my life, to take it away" (1 Kings 19:10).

In one way the powerful prophet's estimation of Israel's spiritual condition was correct and accurate. In truth she had not only rejected the rule of God, but even more alarming had permitted a pagan queen and perverted king to actually attack and demolish all but a fragment of the nation's faith in Jehovah. The altars of the Lord had been razed; the celestial flame had gone out; sacrifices had ceased; the prophets of God had been put to the sword.

In the face of such atrocities Elijah knew full well that ultimately his people would pay an appalling price of pain, suffering and slavery. It is ever thus when men or nations set themselves against God. A day of judgment does descend. Final scores are settled. Sin is dealt with. The irrevocable laws of the Lord are allowed to be unleashed. Then comes sudden devastation upon those who challenge and scoff at God with impunity.

Elijah knew all this. He feared for his nation and for the future. And oddly enough he feared for himself. In fact he was dead sure that only he and he alone now remained true and loyal to the Lord, Jehovah. Somehow, he felt sure that even his own little life was forfeit. And what was he against so many evil men?

What he forgot was that—*one man with God is a majority.*

He also had forgotten—*that God's ways are not man's ways.*

And finally he failed to recall—*the eternal faithfulness of God.*

Elijah's focus and central preoccupation had shifted from God to himself. His faith was no longer fastened on the Lord. Instead, his attention was caught up and centered on the adverse circumstances of his own plight and that of his people.

The result was that events were shaping and molding his mood. They were depressing him down into despair. This was a serious and pitiful reversal for the fierce firebrand.

But it can happen to any of us. As we see the forces of evil in the ascendancy, worldwide, we too can be tempted to despair. We have a choice, however. Either we can mold and influence the world by our faith and confidence in Christ or we can allow the world to compress us into melancholy moods, despair and doubt as we muse upon our own petty self-interests.

The word of the Lord to Elijah at this point was: "Go out and stand on the mount of God in his presence." In other words, "Elijah, get out of your cave of self-pity. You have returned to the old womb of mother earth for safety and security. Get out of there. Be reborn. Emerge again into the full light and splendor of your Savior. See again what God can do!"

Elijah was slow to respond. He lingered in the enfolding gloom and darkness, reluctant to return to the bright light and dazzling intensity of the sun outside.

So a sudden, violent, rushing wind swept across the ridges. It roared through the canyons and over the craggy crest of the rock ramparts. Stone and boulders were loosened from their sockets in the slopes. They crashed down one upon another, loosening and shattering other slabs. All of them together avalanched down the sides of Sinai in great clouds of dust and debris.

It was a fearsome display of nature, but the Lord was not in the wind, even though often his Spirit is likened to the wind.

Then followed an eerie earthquake. For Elijah this earthquake on the mountain was especially terrifying. At any moment great cracks could develop in his cave. Slabs of rock could be shaken from its roof that would crush him to death in their fall. Huge earth movements could crumble the peaks and send down gigantic rock slides that would inter him in a mountain tomb, unknown to anyone but God himself.

It was a terrifying prospect, but the forlorn prophet still felt safer in his cave than to come out and face the fury of the wind or shaking earth. No, God was not in the earthquake either, though often it had been declared he shook heaven and earth.

Then there was a furious fire. It was really more than a brush fire. True, it was a fire that consumed the brush and grass and any vegetation that struggled to survive on the dry slopes of Mount Sinai.

But it was also an electrical display of dry lightning that flashed and flared from crag to crag. Its brilliance lit up the entire dark interior of Elijah's dark cave, but God was not in the fire, even though all through history he often chose to reveal himself in the form of a celestial flame.

When the wind had dropped and the earth ceased to tremble, when the fire had died, there was utter stillness on the mount. And in the intensity of the awesome silence came a still, small voice.

It was the voice of God.

In response to it Elijah wrapped his soiled and dusty mantle about his haggard face and went to stand at the entrance to the cave.

What the wind, the earthquake and the fire could not do, the still, small voice achieved. Elijah was being delivered at last from darkness to light, from death to life, from despair to the love and presence of his God.

We should pause here a moment to reflect on the events of this dramatic day. Furious winds, earth-shaking quakes, fearsome electrical storms were all enough surely to convince Elijah this was God at work. But it was not. Three times it is declared emphatically God was not in the wind, the earthquake, nor in the fire.

In our day Christians everywhere are impressed and captivated by the great winds of change blowing through the church. They are stirred by the shaking experiences of current events. They are mesmerized by the fire and electrical display of so-called special miracles. But is God in them?

It was the still, small voice that drew Elijah back out to the light. It was the intense inner conviction of God's Spirit speaking to the deep intuition of Elijah's spirit, whereby he knew assuredly: *God is in this place!*

And lest the light of the glory of the presence of Jehovah should blind his weary eyes he wrapped his cloak around his head to shield his face from the splendor of the divine effulgence.

Moses had come down off this same mountain, his face aglow with the glory of God. He too had to wrap a veil about his head because of that brightness that so deeply stirred his brethren. They knew he had met God in this mount. So too, now, had Elijah. But he was all alone. There was no other human eye to witness the total transformation.

Again came the searching, stabbing, searing question: *"Elijah—what are you doing here?"*

This time the desert firebrand was not crouched in the dark confines of his cave. He was standing erect, alert, open to a word from heaven, in the bright light of the open mountainside.

In utter consistency and absolute honesty, word for word, Elijah gave exactly the same reply the second time that he did the first. He was not a devious man. In his dealings with God, he did not put up smoke screens of excuses. What he said he meant. His no was no! His yes was yes! He was totally sincere, utterly authentic.

Here he stood again, as of old, the servant of God, standing before his Master, awaiting the word of command. The events on the mountain were the catalyst that again brought him back into intimate communion with the Lord. His days of defeat were over. His hours of despair had been dissipated. His descent into the desperation of discouragement was halted, turned around. He had heard from heaven again. The Lord was with him. All was well once more. There was work to do for God. He was ready to carry out his commands.

If a man of Elijah's caliber could become so downcast, it is apparent that the same can happen to anyone of us. The sin of self-pity is perhaps the most heinous in God's view. It means we simply don't believe God is managing our lives satisfactorily. We feel sorry for ourselves. In so doing we insult our Lord.

The route back from this black pit of despair is not by running from God or circumstances. Nor is it by exciting and ecstatic experiences similar to a great wind, earthquake or fire. It is to hear again the still, small voice of God's Spirit speaking to us through his Word.

The person who truly wants to hear from God will do so. The individual prepared and ready to respond to God's Spirit will be spoken to by the word of the Lord. The man or woman alert and eager to carry out Christ's commands will find communion with him to be very personal, very private yet also very profound.

To hear God implies three basic fundamental facts.

1) I recognize it is God, very God speaking to me through his own Word by his own Spirit.

2) I respond to his Word in faith. This is to have complete confidence in his commands and his character, to the point where I am prepared to act.

3) I run, without excuse, delay or debate, to do the thing God requests. I simply say, "Yes, Lord, whatever your wish or will, here I am to cooperate and comply with it."

Such was precisely Elijah's position at this point. He was fully prepared to go anywhere, do anything, be of any service. It is little wonder he was immediately invested with enormous divine responsibilities under God. In fact, the impact of the prophet's life would now be extended far beyond the borders and boundaries of his own nation.

The instant God diverts an individual's attention from his or her own petty problems and self-centered little interests, to the great power of his own person, there are potentials for enormous exploits under the impetus of God's energy. Most of us block the movement of God's Spirit not only in our own lives, but also in the world at large, by our own selfish intransigence.

The hour that Elijah crawled out of his cave of self-pity and sad introspection was a turning point in his walk with God. As he stood erect on the great mount in full view of his God, his eyes were lifted to see far horizons of exciting new adventures. The Lord still had noble assignments for his servant. They would take the desert firebrand as far as distant Damascus in Syria. This alone was a desert trek of about 500 miles that eclipsed any expedition he had yet made.

He was appointed to anoint Hazael king over Syria. God was using Elijah to bring a new royal dynasty into a foreign nation. Ultimately that nation would be used of God to scourge and chasten Israel severely for her repudiation of Jehovah. Not in vain, or unheard, had been Elijah's protests to the Lord about Israel's perverseness. His great concern for the glory of his God in the lives of his people had not gone unheeded.

We do well to remind ourselves again and again in the midst of both national and international upheavals that ultimately it is the sovereignty of our God that decides who shall have authority in the earth. *Read carefully Romans 13:1–7 and Isaiah 40:12–31*.

In this case Israel, a nation which had despised and rejected its Redeemer, would not go unpunished. In due course there would be dire retribution made upon this rebellious and stubborn people. And Elijah himself was to play a most significant role in those excruciating events, since it was he who was to anoint the new king of Syria, Israel's archenemy.

Similarly in the case of his own nation's royal household Elijah was given responsibility to terminate the awful tyranny of Ahab and Jezebel. Their dreadful days were numbered. The end was already in view for the evil rule of this perverse pair. The wickedness of their ways, the hardness of their hearts, the deception of their false deities would come crashing to a cataclysmic end.

It has been well stated that the mills of God's justice in the earth may appear to grind very slowly. But they also grind very relentlessly. What is more, they grind remorselessly in pulverizing the arrogant.

None of Ahab's progeny would ever enjoy a prolonged reign on their father's throne. His heirs would be cut off from power. None of his offspring would ever come to occupy a place of enduring prominence in Israel. Just as surely and decisively as God terminated Saul's evil reign over Israel, so Ahab's would end in disaster for his dynasty.

Elijah was instructed to go and anoint the fierce and formidable Jehu as the new king in Israel. He would replace the reprobate who now ruled this wretched, ragtag nation. One day soon, the Syrians would slay Ahab in battle, and the stray dogs in the streets of

Samaria would lick his blood from the very ground where he had so arrogantly subverted God's chosen people.

A no less terrible fate would befall his fierce wife Jezebel. At the ferocious command of Jehu, who usurped her husband's throne, she would be flung down from the upper palace windows to be crushed on the streets of her wretched city. There the horses of passing chariots would trample her prostrate form to a pulp. She, though once a queen, would not even receive a proper burial, for nothing more than the mutilated palms of her hands and severed soles of her feet would be found after the grizzly ordeal.

No, indeed, there may well be those who scoff, lampoon and jeer at God. But always, always, always, he has the last word; he directs the final action in the drama of a man's days and destiny.

In his own place and stead, Elijah was instructed to anoint Elisha as his worthy successor. This young prophet would eventually achieve twice as much as Elijah had accomplished. It was all part of the ebb and flow of the tide of God's own Spirit at work in Elijah's world of chaos and confusion.

As a final encouragement to the powerful prophet, the Lord assured him that there still remained in Israel at least 7,000 sturdy souls who had never succumbed to the deception of Baal or Ashteroth. Elijah was not the only one faithful to Jehovah. His estimation of the depravity of his day was more pessimistic than was justified by the facts. He had misjudged the gravity of his times.

This, too, is often true of us. We think things are bleaker than they really are. Often we fail to count on the greatness of our God. We forget, sometimes that he is very much at work in the world behind the scenes. Things really are not always quite as black as they appear. God is still sovereign in the universe. His purposes do come to pass.

20

Elijah Finds Elisha

The intimate encounter on Sinai between Jehovah and Elijah reestablished a right relationship between them. No longer did Elijah feel alone and abandoned in his service to God. Once again the Lord had demonstrated his integrity and trustworthiness. He was ever present to direct and energize the powerful prophet in the appointments and responsibilities entrusted to him.

It was perfectly valid to say again that "It is God which worketh in you both to will and to do of his good pleasure" (Phil. 2:13).

Elijah might well have preferred to remain in semi-seclusion on the mount. He may have legitimately felt that he had been exposed to enough danger and hardship to last him the rest of his life. He may have been convinced that he now deserved a more placid pace of events and more tranquil tempo of life.

Still there was work to do down in the lowlands of his day. There were assignments to carry out for God. There were lives he had to touch. There were places he had to go; words he had to speak. Yes, there yet remained one more traumatic encounter with the wretched Ahab. Despite all that God had done to display himself on Carmel, the monarch remained an irascible despot.

Elijah's interlude on Mount Horeb (Sinai) very much resembled the experience our Lord, Peter, James and John had on Mount Hermon. There in the presence of his Master's magnificent transfiguration, Peter's impulse was to erect three suitable sanctuaries where all of them together with Moses and Elijah could remain on the mount.

But it was not to be. It never is God's intention for his special people to remain long in the rarefied atmosphere of the mountaintop. Our Lord knew that a desperate father and his demon-possessed child awaited his return down on the plain at the foot of the mountain.

There still remained the remorse, the sin, the pain, the tears, the sorrow, the tragedy and pathos of a broken world below.

God does not indefinitely extend the mountaintop experiences of even his most devout servants. Moses came down off this same burning, smoking Sinai to hear the mad music, and to discover the devilish dancing of his reprobate people. They had made themselves a golden calf as a gruesome idol while he was gone. But for the prophet's incredible intervention on their part, all of Israel would then have perished for their perverseness.

No, God does not withdraw his prophets of power into the seclusion of their Sinais. Instead, he sends them out to speak, to serve, to witness to a world out of joint.

Jesus himself declared emphatically to his tiny handful of followers just before his own arrest by the mob who would lynch him in the garden of Gethsemane: "As the Father hath sent me, so send I you . . ." to minister to men in darkness, debauchery and despair.

So Elijah set off north again. There would be hundreds of miles of burning sands and barren rock to traverse. He would know dreadful weariness and intense strain and awful thirst. But go he must, no matter the personal cost, the personal privation.

On his return to Israel he quickly found Elisha, the youth chosen of God to succeed him as prophet in Israel. Elisha came from a very wealthy family. Few country men in ancient Israel could boast of more than one pair of oxen to do the plowing on their tiny plot of land. Elisha's father owned twelve yoke of oxen. There were twelve teams and twelve drivers in the field, each working in tandem behind the next.

The recent rains had softened the soil. It was suitable for plowing and planting. So all the plows were at work. At the very tail end of the twelve teams came Elisha. His was the worst working position in the field, for there he had to cope with all the dust and dirt raised in clouds by the plowmen and teams ahead of him. Obviously he was a young man accustomed to work. Hardened by discipline within his own home, humble in heart, he was willing to labor in the most lowly position for his parents.

Without any special fanfare or formalities, Elijah strode across the plowed ground toward Elisha. Whipping off his own mantle, already soiled with dust and dirt from his desert travels, he tossed it around the young plowman's shoulders.

Naked, but for his brief loincloth and the leather belt that bound it around his waist, Elijah strode on across the field of fresh-turned clods. He scarcely paused in stride. His sandaled feet had carried him across hundreds of miles of desert wastes, and he still had to reach Damascus, at least another two hundred miles further north.

Elisha shouted to his team to halt. With Elijah's strange and unfamiliar mantle billowing about his shoulders he tore off across the plowed ground to catch up with the shaggy, desert firebrand.

"Elijah, Elijah—" he burst out breathlessly as he overtook the older man in full stride. "Let me simply kiss my parents good-by and I will follow you!"

The flaming eyed prophet turned in his tracks. He stood there like a stark statue, stripped of his robe, looking wistfully at the young farm boy. "By all means, Elisha, go and do what you must do. My assignment from Jehovah has been carried out."

As the young Elisha looked full into the blazing, burning eyes of the powerful prophet he knew assuredly that he, of all his people, had been selected, chosen with care, and called to special service. This was no pantomime performance. Elijah and Elisha were not playing games. This was a call for keeps. This was a commissioning under divine command. This was to move from the civilian ranks into a combat corps for God.

Young Elisha was not insensitive to the movement and message of the Spirit of God active in Elijah. He had been one of the multitudes massed on Mount Carmel. He had seen the pathetic false prophets of Baal fail to call down fire from heaven. Awestruck, he had stood there watching Elijah lay up the altar of stones. He had watched entranced as the ditch was dug around it; the wood laid in order; the ox butchered and quartered; the flesh placed upon the wood. He was deeply stirred as he saw the whole soaked again and again with sea water.

Something deep within Elisha stirred as the powerful prophet raised his gaunt, sunburned face toward the blazing skies entreating Jehovah to hear from heaven. It was a burning, yearning petition torn from the heart of a man right with his God. Then the fire fell. Then the altar stones, the wood, the water, the flesh and even the soil went up in smoke and steam.

What a spectacle! All the crowd fell flat on their faces crying out aloud, "Jehovah, he is the Lord. The Lord, he is God!"

Then and there, perhaps, Elisha vowed secretly that if ever he were called of God to serve as his spokesman, he would not hesitate a second. What greater honor could come to a son of the soil, a son of Israel?

Now that moment had come. Now the call was clear. Now the fork in life's road was here. Things would not be, could not be, ever the same again. He had reached his Rubicon.

Leaving Elijah, the young fellow ran back to his patient yoke of oxen standing in the field. He pulled the crude plow from the hard ground and flung it on its side. Then shouting to his team, he drove them home across the field dragging the wooden plow behind them.

Elisha's action had an electrifying effect on his whole family. In between gasps of excitement he told them about what Elijah had done. There was no denying his divine call. In swift succession he unyoked his team; butchered both beasts; smashed up their wooden yoke and plow into firewood; then he used the fuel to prepare a farewell feast for his family and friends.

It was all done with a minimum of delay. Nothing would deflect Elisha from his determination to do God's will. Nothing could divert him from his call to service. Nothing would remain to draw him back again from following his new-found Master. He was burning all his bridges behind him. There would never again be his favorite oxen to drive across this land he loved. Never again would he feel the yoke or the thrill of the plow handles in his strong hands. There would never again be the sweet fragrance of freshly turned earth in these fields to tantalize his nostrils.

In a single, sudden, severe stroke of severance Elisha gave up his family, his friends, his farm, his fervent love for the land, his whole future. It was an incredible act of self-sacrifice for one so young. But Elijah's mantle had fallen upon him. The hand of God had gripped his heart. The word of the Lord had captivated his will and taken it under full command.

He was ready and eager to go wherever God wished.

Are we surprised that God would eventually use Elisha to accomplish such great exploits in Israel? Are we surprised to see this young man so swiftly assume the rigorous role of a prophet to his people? Elijah had found himself the man of God's appointment. He would prove to be the finest protegé any prophet was ever privileged to have in his company. From now on Elijah the veteran and Elisha the trainee would be inseparable friends, until the day God called one of them away to still higher service.

Elisha exemplifies for us clearly the sort of person for whom God is eternally seeking. He is that responsive individual, open, available, eager to respond positively to the call of God. It is such people who, in the hand of God, become the ones who achieve mighty things in the economy of Christ. There is no debate, no delay. They simply step out to do God's will . . . *now!*

21

Elijah in Naboth's Vineyard

Elijah and his young companion, Elisha, appear to drop out of public view for something like six years. We are not told where they went or what they did during this long interval of obscurity. Perhaps Elijah was directed by God to establish some sort of training centers where young men, out of the 7,000 who had never bowed the knee to Baal, could be prepared for service to Jehovah. In any case, at a later date reference is made to groups of prophets where both Elijah and Elisha were well known.

In any event life for Israel as a nation continued to be stormy and tempestuous during this time. It scarcely could be otherwise with such a degenerate monarch as Ahab and his wicked queen Jezebel. The nation came under attack from Syria, its ancient enemy in the north. After cruel threats and impossible demands for the total surrender of Ahab's silver, gold, sons and daughters, Ben-hadad and his armies attacked Ahab.

There were two tremendous battles. The first was in

the hilly country not far from Jezreel. Here God granted the young, inept Israelis great victory despite their inexperience in warfare. Quite obviously it was a supernatural triumph whereby the Lord endeavored to demonstrate once more that he was in fact God very God in Israel.

About a year later Ben-hadad again marshaled his forces for a second assault against Ahab. This time his advisers suggested that the battle be fought down on the plains. In their gross ignorance, they assured Ben-hadad that the God of Israel was essentially and only a God of the hills. If they engaged the Israeli army in the lowlands they could be sure of victory. Apparently the presence of Jehovah with the young army of Israel had not gone unnoticed by the Syrian commanders.

The outcome of the second battle on the plains was an even greater victory for Ahab than the first in the hills. Ben-hadad himself was taken captive. The power of the Syrians was shattered. And Jehovah had again shown that he could deliver Israel from her foes anywhere at any time.

One of the young prophets rebuked Ahab for sparing Ben-hadad's life. He was told that because he had so willingly compromised with the Syrians, subsequent serious repercussions would fall upon both him and his nation. As usual with Ahab he was outraged and went into a deep sulk over the reprimand. He was not the sort of ruler to accept any divine directions from the Lord God who had granted his armies such amazing victories.

Ahab never seemed able to learn anything from the ebb and flow of circumstantial events around him. Even though these had been ordered and arranged of God they seemed to have no perceptible impact on his perverse and petulant nature. The Lord had sent Elijah nearly ten years before to warn him of his wicked ways. The dreadful famine had come to decimate the country. Then followed the remarkable and fantastic flame of celestial fire on Carmel. After that came the great rains to refresh the land. Now he had been granted two glorious military victories. Yet all of it seemed of absolutely no avail in turning the heart of this tough and taciturn tyrant toward God.

In looking over the highlights of his life, we can only marvel at the amazing patience and perseverance of God in dealing with such a dreadful individual. Surely the Spirit of the Most High, like the hound of heaven, pursues petulant people; perverse people; proud people with incredible tenacity. God in his grace declines to destroy any stubborn souls as long as there is even a shred of hope that they might yet repent, reverse their ways and turn to him for newness of life.

Despite all that the Lord had done, Ahab and his vicious queen drifted steadily downward into debauchery. The end finally came in their conduct over a tiny plot of ground near the palace that belonged to a poor peasant named Naboth.

Ahab decided that Naboth's little vineyard would make an ideal herb garden. It was handy to the royal kitchen and there the delectable vegetables and herbs used to garnish his dishes could be grown with ease. The king spoke to Naboth about the matter. He offered to buy it outright or to give the fellow another piece of royal ground in exchange.

Naboth declined the king's offer, not to be difficult, but because of the Hebrew tradition, ordained of God, which forbade such transactions (see Num. 36:7–9). Again, as usual, Ahab was furious in his frustration. Sinking down into a malevolent mood, he went into his royal chambers, lay down in a stubborn sulk, much like a spoiled child, refusing to eat.

Jezebel, hearing about what happened, was not about to have her husband's covetousness thwarted by so small a thing as a poor farmer's intransigence. There were quick, cruel and cunning ways to remove and liquidate anyone with the temerity to stand against the regal whims of his royal highness.

She arranged a royal fast, which in fact was a false charade, at which Naboth was to be the royal guest of special honor. Little did the poor fellow know he was being prepared like a lamb for slaughter. In the midst of the performance, false accusations were brought against Naboth. He was charged with blasphemy against God and king. For such outrages he was dragged outside the city walls to be stoned. His body, bruised and smashed with the stones and boulders hurled by his own compatriots, was left a mangled corpse in the place where later Ahab's own blood would be licked up by stray dogs.

But Jezebel did not know this in her passing moment of pride and passion. She rushed in to Ahab, roused him from his sulking mood, and bade him take the tiny plot of ground on which his hard and haughty heart had been set. It had been easy for her to engineer this dreadful deed. And certainly Ahab never lifted a finger to forbid her devilish designs.

Instead, selfish, blind, haughty soul that he was, the king strolled down to see the land to which he now laid claim. His actions had all been under the most intense divine scrutiny. For as he walked nonchalantly amongst the vines, kicking up the fertile soil with his royal feet, relishing the thought of the leeks and lentils it would provide for his plate, Elijah suddenly confronted him.

"You have found me out again—my enemy!" the enraged king growled at Elijah. For almost seven years the eyes of the two men had not met. For almost seven years Elijah had been living in relative obscurity. For almost seven years he had been forgotten.

But now here he was back again. Back to badger and

berate the king just when he thought he had this plot of ground in his possession. Back to point out the peril of his position as king of Israel. Back to proclaim the terrible and terrifying verdict of God upon him and his queen.

Elijah had been sent with a word of judgment from the Lord. The awesome, amazing, incredible patience of God had been strained to its breaking point by the sins of Ahab and Jezebel. Nothing they had thought, felt or done, had passed unnoticed. Every detail of their conversation and conduct had been under the continual scrutiny of God's Spirit. At last it had dawned upon Ahab's dull conscience that nothing, ever, anywhere, at any time under any conditions could ever be concealed from divine observation. He had been found out. And it left him speechless.

The rather remarkable thing is that most of us human beings are really not much different from Ahab in this regard. In our naive stupidity we assume that because we can at times conceal our motives, thoughts, intentions and wrongdoing from other human beings, we can likewise conceal them from God. This is utter folly. It is the utmost absurdity. It is total blindness to divine truth.

The special revelation of God's Word to us is that he does know every intimate detail of our lives. Every move we make, every thought we think, every intention we entertain is wide open to his view. He knows us better than we know ourselves. For confirmation of this one need only read such passages as Psalm 139.

Ahab's covetousness; his desire to take that which was not rightfully his; his acquiescence to his wife's diabolical death plan; his indifference to the murder of an innocent man; his refusal to reverse the course of events; his placid submission to the scandalous designs of his devilish queen; his selfishness in seizing a poor man's property—all these were abhorrent to God. He, the Almighty, was fully aware of all that went on. Now it would have to stop.

So Elijah, who so long ago had fled in fear from this same spot, was back to declare God's apocalyptic judgments upon this cruel couple. This day Elijah did not stand in fear or apprehension. Instead, he stood strong and sure in the Spirit of his Lord. Like tremendous hammer blows falling upon his anvil-hard heart, Ahab listened with bowed head:

"Ahab, you have sold out completely to sin and evil.
Ahab, all your male offspring will be cut off and perish.
Ahab, your royal lineage is to terminate.
Ahab, your blood will be licked up by dogs in the same spot where Naboth's blood was spilled.
Ahab, your wife Jezebel's corpse shall be consumed by dogs in the city of Jezreel.
Ahab, your sins have brought their own ultimate disaster upon you and your dynasty."

It demanded great courage and confident certitude for Elijah to deliver such severe imprecations to his monarch. Only a man closely attuned to the Spirit of the Living Lord would dare to be so brave.

It takes enormous integrity to be a spokesman for God. A world set against him never welcomes the tough truths entrusted to fearless, flaming prophets. More often than not the first reaction of those rebuked is simply to slay the spokesman; still his voice; silence his warning; sever his service.

Ahab and Jezebel may have intended to do this once before to Elijah. But not this time. The queen may have threatened to take the prophet's life just as she had arranged the murder of Naboth. But not this time. Both Ahab and Jezebel might well have preferred never to see the flaming desert firebrand again. But not this time. He would be back.

In the meantime Ahab saw himself for the first time as he really was. He saw something of the awfulness of his own wrongdoing. He saw that in submitting to his own selfish designs and desires he had literally enslaved himself to sin. He saw that he was in very fact not a free king to act in any way he wished. Rather he was a mere man shackled to his own self-centered lusts by chains forged in the heated fury of his own selfish behavior. Of course his wife and queen had been no help to him. In fact she had been like the bellows that blew the flame of his passions and perverseness into ever greater heat and fury.

It is a deluded fool who believes that because he can do as he wishes, go where he likes, behave as he may choose, that he is fully free. The opposite is true, for until God, in Christ, comes upon men and women to set them free from the bondage to their old self-centeredness, they remain slaves to sin, slaves to themselves. Only the coming of God in mercy sets a soul free from the folly of the old ways, to walk with him in humility.

Fortunately for Ahab on this dreadful day, the truth of his spiritual state broke through the dreadful deadness of his sin-saturated soul. For the first time he saw himself as he really was: naked, stripped, fully exposed in all his evil before a righteous, patient, gracious God.

Despite what Jezebel might say, think or do, despite what all his subject people might say, Ahab tore his royal robes from his shoulders. He picked up fistfuls of the dust from Naboth's plot of ground, flinging them in remorse over his head and body. He exchanged his royal tunic for a sack. Then covered in ashes he lay down in broken repentance, refusing to eat or drink, humbled before God and men.

This was a tremendous act of contrition and remorse. All of Israel saw their king in mourning for his own grievous misdemeanor. Even when the days of fasting were over, Ahab now walked softly, quietly before the Lord. Gone was the arrogance, the petulance, the bombasity of his old life style.

Again Elijah came to the royal palace. This time, for the first time, he came bearing good news. Just as Jehovah had seen every secret sin, so now he had also seen Ahab's sincere humiliation of heart and remorse of spirit.

"Ahab, you have been given a reprieve. The dreadful disasters predicted for your posterity will not fall during your lifetime, but after your death."

The penitent king and the powerful prophet were never to meet again. For ten years Elijah's faithfulness and fortitude for the Lord had made its impact on the royal household. Finally Ahab had been brought to a place of repentance. Elijah's work was done.

What was not ended was the ongoing influence of Ahab's wicked ways. Ultimately, sin always brings forth its own bitter fruit. And even though it be confessed, forgiven and forgotten by God, there is eventually a day when the practical out-workings of that wrong have their effect in human society.

No person lives an isolated life like a remote island in a great sea. Each of our lives touches and transforms those around us, either for good or for evil. And the ongoing consequences of a man's misdeeds can and do have an impact upon his family, friends and offspring. This was to happen in Ahab's case. We cannot sin with impunity. Subsequently and ultimately, either in this life or else in the next, retribution must be made for the wrong. After Ahab's death terrible calamities would overtake his children as foretold by the fiery prophet.

Indeed all that Elijah decreed regarding the gruesome end of both this king and queen did come to pass precisely as he predicted. Ahab was slain in battle and his blood, when flushed from the floor of his battle chariot, was licked up by the dogs where Naboth's blood now stained the soil outside this cruel city's walls.

As for Jezebel, her body never even received a royal burial. Flung from a palace window, she was crushed under the trampling hooves of Jehu's fierce chariot horses. By the time the scrawny, scavenging dogs of Jezreel were done with her corpse, only her mangled hands and feet remained as a grim reminder of her cruel rule.

Only fools flaunt God. Only the self-deluded indulge their cynicism against Christ. Only the skeptic says in his heart of hearts, *"There is no God!"*

22

Elijah and Ahaziah

After Ahab died, the subject kingdom of Moab lying in the sunburned wastes east of Jordan, rebelled against Israel. They had been taxed with producing 100,000 lamb fleeces and 100,000 ram skins annually. This had gone on since King David's army had subdued them about 46 years before.

Now they had had enough. When the weak-willed, profligate son of Ahab and Jezebel tried to assume power in his wicked father's place, the desert colony decided to break away. For the weak-kneed Ahaziah this was a disturbing development.

Either in agitation over the rebellion of Moab, or in a drunken stupor he fell through the lattice work encircling the palace balcony. Crashing to the ground below he was seriously injured. His suffering was so excruciating that he decided to seek supernatural advice as to whether or not he would recover.

Instead of sending for one of the prophets of Jehovah he instructed his servants to go and consult with the diabolical pagan deity, *Baalzebub*. This was the dreadful god of the dung heap, the god of flies held in special esteem by the Philistines. He was worshiped as the supreme ruler of the occult world of evil spirits.

Steeped in the perverse paganism of his parents, the foolish Ahaziah had obviously learned absolutely nothing from the great events of Israel's famine, the celestial fire on Carmel, or the slaughter of Baal's prophets. Like a boar returning to wallow in its mud, so Ahab's family returned again to the awful false gods of Canaan. Ahaziah acted as though he knew nothing but the evil perversion of his parents.

The messengers sent to Baalzebub were scarcely started on their mad mission when Elijah intercepted them. He had been given divine instructions to do so. His sudden appearance, all unshaven, long-haired, burned brown as old oak by desert sun, girt only in wild animal skins, startled the royal servants.

"Is there no God in Israel"—Elijah challenged them, his eyes ablaze—*"that you must consult with such a pagan deity as Baalzebub?"*

The powerful prophet's sudden appearance was a shock. His question was not even answered. There was no debate or discussion. The king's servants knew only that they stood in the presence of a fierce and flaming spokesman for God.

"Go back to the palace and tell Ahaziah he shall surely die!" With those terse, sharp, severe words Elijah was gone, and the emissaries fled back to report to the royal household.

Ahaziah, when told what the prophet who intercepted them looked like, exclaimed in commingled anger and awe, *"It is Elijah—the Tishbite."* The flaming firebrand had not been seen for four years since the dreadful day he confronted his father in Naboth's vineyard. Ahab's deep repentance in sackcloth seemed not to have touched the besotted soul of this stubborn son of Baal.

He would never bend the knee to Elijah. Never would he submit to his spirited defense of Jehovah. He would never come under God's control. No, a thousand times no! Elijah was his enemy. Elijah was the thorny threat to his wicked ways. Elijah would have to go. Like his vicious, vengeful mother Jezebel, Ahaziah would wipe out this wild-eyed desert prophet.

In his fury he ordered one of his army captains with a contingent of fifty men to go out and capture Elijah in his mountain hideaway. Obviously they knew the desert prophet's favorite rocky retreat.

This time Elijah did not run for his life. There would not be a repeat performance of his former flight into despair and despondency. Instead he simply stood his ground in great dignity and defiance of evil.

"The king says for you to come down, O man of God!" The surly captain shouted at him.

Calmly Elijah retorted: *"If I am indeed God's man, then let fire come down and consume your whole contingent."*

And it did.

The deed was done.

The fifty-one men simply disappeared.

When word got back to Ahaziah of what had happened, instead of humbling himself before the Lord, he became doubly indignant and sent off a second troop of fifty men and their captain to apprehend Elijah.

Obviously the second commander shared the arrogant ignorance of Ahaziah his king, for he shouted impatiently at Elijah, *"Come down quickly!"* His monarch had to be obeyed at once.

Again fire fell.

The whole contingent perished.

And word was sent back a second time of the disaster.

The incredible stupidity and insolent pride of this sullen son of Ahab are almost beyond belief, for he would not relent. He sent off a third captain with fifty fighting men to capture the fiery prophet.

Fortunately for all concerned, this third military

man was an individual of integrity, courtesy and humble spirit. He had sense enough to recognize that his king had set himself against God. And though he was caught in the middle, by submitting to the sovereignty of Jehovah and bowing humbly before Elijah he could save himself, his men and the whole sticky situation.

Casting himself upon Elijah's mercy he begged him on bended knee to withhold the fire that would otherwise consume them. The response was remarkable. Elijah agreed to go with him. Reassured by the angel that he need not be afraid, the powerful prophet proceeded for the last time in his cataclysmic career to enter the king's palace.

Without hesitation or apology the fierce desert firebrand faced the furious monarch and spoke these solemn words: *"Because you have behaved as though there is no God in Israel, and sought instead the services of Baalzebub (God's archenemy), you shall surely die!"*

And die Ahaziah did.

His short and stormy reign lasted less than two years.

It was the disastrous conclusion to a dynasty steeped in pagan worship and devilish debauchery.

The pronouncement made by the Lord God Almighty to Elijah on Mount Sinai had come to pass exactly as had been predicted.

All through the long, desperate, difficult years of his service to Jehovah, Elijah had confronted the evil of his times with enormous fortitude. Over and over he had challenged the wickedness of the monarchy. He had spoken aloud for his God. Again and again it had well nigh cost him his very life. Only because Elijah feared God so much did he dare to fear men so little.

Yet amid all of these stirring events and exciting episodes, Elijah was locked in battle with more than just men and monarchs. His contest was not only with corrupt rulers and decadent despots. He was essentially in combat with all of the forces of evil arraigned against God.

It is important for us to see this in its true light and proper perspective. Nearly a thousand years later Paul, another great spokesman for the Lord, who also had faced the fury and injustice of monarchs, rulers, and corrupt government, put it this way: "*We are not fighting against human beings but against the wicked spiritual forces in the heavenly world, the rulers, authorities, and cosmic powers of this dark age. So put on God's armour now! Then when the evil day comes, you will be able to resist the enemy's attacks; and after fighting to the end, you will still hold your ground*" (Eph. 6:12,13, *Good News Bible*).

Too many of us assume naively that only certain men and women are wicked. We feel that our opponents are often just disillusioned or misguided individuals. Too frequently we feel sure that the Christian is only confronted by other belligerent human beings. Not so. The supernatural forces at work in the cosmos control masses of humanity. What great battles go on in the unseen realm are not always known to us, but they do have their repercussions in the ongoing affairs of human history.

This Elijah knew, understood and faced with formidable fortitude. He was not just confronting an evil king, a wicked queen or their despicable son. He was facing the full fury of the false gods of Baal, Ashteroth and Baalzebub, as well as their host of false prophets.

From the perspective of the historical scriptural record left to us, we might be led to think that Elijah's life story was that of a solitary soul struggling against the evil tendencies of his times. In part that is true. But in greater part we are compelled to conclude that Elijah was by no means alone. God had assured him unmistakably on Sinai that there were 7,000 other stalwart souls who had never bowed to Baal, never submitted to Ashteroth. No, he was not in this struggle single-handed.

What Elijah does stand for in all of his magnificent splendor is the courage and commitment of a man who was determined to be faithful to his God. His relationship to the Lord was very personal, private yet potent! Therein lay the secret of his superb, spiritual strength and endurance.

Throughout this biography of his life every endeavor has been made to show that this fiery fellow was not a super-spiritual saint. He was a man subject to the same discouragements, the same frailties, the same passions as most of us are. Obviously he was even fearful in this last encounter with Ahaziah's commando units. He had to be reassured by the Angel of the Lord that he need not fear men.

If this be true for Elijah, how much more so, then, for most of us? The secret to his astonishing success as God's spokesman and servant was his implicit and prompt compliance with God's commands. Whatever the Lord said, he did. This formidable faith in the total trustworthiness of God saw Elijah perform in a manner most of us would love to emulate.

There really is no reason why that cannot be. God has not changed. His commitments to his people remain constant. His power is still available to any today who will trust him as Elijah did.

23

The Last Trek

The time for Elijah's last earthly trek had come. His remarkable career had been marked by tremendous trips back and forth across the length and breadth of Palestine. He had been a man on the move for God. His fiery exploits and formidable encounters with the forces of evil had taken him from as far north as Damascus in Syria to Mount Sinai in the south; from the deserts east of Jordan to the heights of Carmel overlooking the blue Mediterranean in the west.

Like the fierce Sirocco winds that swept across this weary land, Elijah had swept across the life of his tired times under the powerful impulse of God's own Spirit. He had been the supreme counteracting force of his generation opposed to the decadence and degradation of his day.

The Spirit of God ever searches for such souls. He is eager to invade and invest any human spirit open and available to his overtures. He will pick them up, energize, inspire and empower them to fulfill the purposes of God upon the planet.

But now Elijah's exploits under God were all but fully completed. He knew with the deep intuition of his spirit that the time for his last trek had come. There were no more Ahabs, Jezebels, Obadiahs, Ahaziahs or pursuing officers to face. His feet would take him gently at last to visit with his friends amongst the sons of the prophets whom Jezebel had slaughtered. There would be brief but fitting farewells. Then there was the Jordan to cross for a last time. After that—well, after that who knew what would happen? All he really knew for sure was that at long last his work in the world was done and he was heading "home."

For ten long, full, tough years Elijah and Elisha, his young protegé, had been inseparable companions. Wherever Elijah went, Elisha followed him, faithful as his own shadow. During those ten years of internship under the fiery, formidable prophet, Elisha had matured mightily into a vigorous man of God.

Month after month Elisha had not only served the powerful prophet in a physical way, but even more important, had literally "sat at his feet" in spiritual instruction. All the great insights into the secrets of walking with God had been shared between the young man and his aged mentor.

Over the ten-year period Elijah came to be in truth a father to Elisha. When the young farmer kissed his parents good-by, for good, he had found a new father in Elijah: One whom he adored, admired and loved completely with every fiber of his own forceful manhood.

Just as the souls of Ruth and Naomi, and David and Jonathan had been knit together into a single purpose, so Elijah and Elisha were completely one in spirit, one in mind, one in their purpose to serve Jehovah God.

This gives us a remarkable insight into the character of Elijah. Ordinarily men of his type can be tough, hard, abrasive individuals. They are often "loners" who find it well nigh impossible to adapt themselves to other lesser people. Their driving dispositions, undeviating commitment to a cause, steellike determination, unflinching faith and rigid self-discipline make them rather difficult people.

Yet Elijah obviously was not like this. He had lived in humble gratitude with the widow woman for three years. He had lived in gentle harmony with young Elisha for ten years. In fact, despite his formidable character he was dearly loved.

So on this last morning together, when Elijah urged his young friend to stay behind at Gilgal, high in the hills north of Bethel, Elisha declined. He, too, somehow sensed that Elijah's day of departure had come. Nothing or no one could possibly persuade him to be parted from the powerful prophet a solitary instant before it was absolutely necessary.

"No, no, Elijah," he protested. *"As long as God lives, and you are alive, I will not leave you!"* He was determined to stay with his beloved master until the last possible moment. Not for a second would he consider leaving the one he loved and honored so intensely.

Perhaps Elijah, in his concern and compassion for his young companion, wished to spare him the agony of a prolonged parting. He looked on the youthful prophet as his very own spiritual son, just as Paul later on was to regard Timothy as his son. At any rate it was apparent to both men that this was to be their last day together.

Together they set off. Their first stop was Bethel. Elijah felt constrained by God's Spirit to go there. He would have a few parting words there for the other young men who, like Elisha, needed encouragement and challenge to carry on God's work. They, too, seemed to know instinctively that this would be their last glimpse of the desert firebrand. Somehow they sensed that the long and intimate friendship between Elijah and Elisha was about to be sundered.

"Do you really realize that today you will lose your master?"

In quiet calmness, Elisha replied that he did in truth know this. He was fully aware of all that would be implied in their parting. He was not unprepared. They need not worry.

Again Elijah looked fondly at his long-time friend and suggested that he stay at Bethel. The name *Bethel* means "the house of God." Here Elisha could feel at home. Here he would have a new circle of companions to ease the pain of their parting, the longing and loneliness of his solitude.

But the doughty Elisha would not hear of it. Some of the fierce stamina, rugged strength and unflinching spirit of the older man had ingrained itself into the younger. He would stick to his hero to the last step, no matter what the cost.

So the two of them pushed on to Jericho. It was downhill most of the way. The trail wound down the steep hills in sharp twists and turns. They took it in full stride and covered the twenty-three miles in a few hours under the blazing sun.

At Jericho there was a repeat performance of what had transpired at Bethel. The same parting with the sons of the prophets who resided in this hot city, the same questions put to Elisha by the novitiates, the same reply, the same request by Elijah that Elisha remain in this pleasant spot whose name, *Jericho,* means, "The place of fragrance."

Jericho was where the date palms and flowering fruit trees, watered from the Jordan, spread their sweet perfumes on the warm air. It would be a comfortable, congenial spot for young Elisha to settle down with other young prophets. It was the sort of place where Elijah was sure Elisha would soon get over his loss after their parting.

But Elisha was adamant. He would not linger here.

He would not leave Elijah no matter where God took him.

Such fortitude and fidelity move us deeply. Here was a young man irrevocably devoted to his teacher, his mentor, his master, his friend, his father. It did not matter how much his own self-denial entailed; he would stay true to Elijah no matter where they went.

Elijah assured him that it was God's intention that he should go on to the Jordan River, leaving the pleasant gardens and groves of Jericho behind. Again Elisha insisted on accompanying him. So they set off across the hot plain toward the distant banks of the muddy river.

Fifty of the young prophets in Jericho were somewhat skeptical that Elisha really knew what he was about. They had queried him closely about the impending parting. But as before, at Bethel, the young protegé reassured them that all was well and they should simply relax. There was no problem. He would just quietly accompany Elijah as they walked on eastward with the glow of the setting sun behind them.

It had been a long day. From Gilgal to Jericho was close to thirty miles and now as the sun sank into the ridges of the western hills, Elijah and Elisha came to the banks of the river that had always cut such a notable and conspicuous path through the life of Israel.

For a short time the two men paused at the same spot where Joshua and his host of two million or more Israelis had crossed this current some 555 years before. At that epic point in the history of their forefathers Joshua had crossed the Jordan from east to west. Now Elijah and Elisha would cross it from west to east.

Fifty of the sons of the prophets had furtively followed the two men. Now they stood at a distance looking on curiously to see what would happen. One never knew what to expect next with Elijah.

Even more important the same youths really did not know the true character of either Elijah or Elisha. They were not aware that during this day God would again demonstrate beyond any doubt how he actually did reside with these two choice and unusual men.

Individuals like Elijah and Elisha are rather rare and unique—seldom found in company. Their kind are so few and far between that only once or twice in any given generation do such men of God appear on the stage of human history. Most of us are a mediocre lot, whose lives are not really aflame, on fire, incandescent with the living Spirit of the Living God.

Whether or not the young Elisha was consciously aware of it or not, the fact remains that what he had seen and encountered in Elijah's spirit, he also sought and longed for in his own spirit. He wanted above everything else not just to be an onlooker like the fifty young prophets. He wanted to be an active participant in the plans, purposes and power of God for his people. This he was determined to have at any price, no matter the personal cost.

Elisha saw himself as Elijah's first-born spiritual son and as such he felt fully entitled to the double portion which was the rightful inheritance of the first-born. Yet he was also astute enough to know that his own strength, his own serenity, his own stability as God's servant could not be vested in Elijah, powerful prophet that he was. No, rather his resources would and must reside in the divine Spirit of the Living God.

Standing there together, looking longingly across the river, both men wondered in just what way Jehovah would see fit to bring their journey together to an end—Jordan was always the "great divide"!

24

The Flaming Farewell

Elijah slipped the dusty, desert-worn mantle from his sunburned shoulders. He stood there beside the slow-moving muddy waters of the Jordan stripped and naked, but for a worn and frayed leather loincloth. He was still the fierce, desert hawk chosen of God some fourteen years before to call Israel back to Jehovah, the Lord. Now he was headed "home."

The powerful prophet's physique was still strong, lean as camel hide, tough as a tamarind tree. His eyes blazed and burned with fierce intensity. Like Moses of old, it could also be said of this nomad, "His eye had not grown dim nor his strength abated." Elijah had never put razor to his beard or locks. Masses of hair, thick, lustrous and waving, crowned his head and swathed his wild rugged features. He was burned leather-brown by wind and weather.

In contrast the young Elisha stood beside him fully garbed and strangely enough, quite bald-headed. It seemed incongruous that he should be the younger of the two famous prophets.

Momentarily Elijah stood poised like a statue staring across the broad expanse of the brooding river. This was the same spot where Joshua, his armies and some 2,000,000 Israeli immigrants had crossed the Jordan five and a half centuries before. The instant the priest's feet had touched the water's edge, the current was held back and the crowd crossed. Elijah's confidence was that God would do the same for him. Jehovah had not changed in 555 years. What he could do for a nation he would gladly do for one man and his friend.

In forthright faith, Elijah rolled up his mantle, symbol of his power and authority under God. With it he struck the river waters. The flowing current held back. Unafraid the two men stepped out into the riverbed and walked across into the desert wastes of the trans-Jordan. They were back in the land of Elijah's birth and boyhood, headed toward the heights of Mount Gilead.

Elijah knew assuredly now that the hour of his own departure was imminent. In a gesture of gentle tenderness and compassion he turned to his faithful young companion: "*Elisha—before I leave you—what special, final favor can I do for you?*"

The young prophet did not hesitate a moment. For a long, long time he had known what it was he longed for more than anything else. He yearned to possess the same power, the same faith, the same fortitude, the same shining spirit that he had seen in Elijah's walk with God. It wasn't his desire just to bask in the afterglow of Elijah's exploits. He refused to rest on the older man's reputation. Nor was he content just to be known as Elijah's companion, protegé and confidante. "*My father,*" Elisha replied, "*pray God that a double portion of the Spirit who has resided with you, reside likewise with me.*"

It was a profound petition. He was not asking for prestige or prominence or personal gain. He was requesting that the presence of God by his Spirit be with him in double measure. He saw himself as

Elijah's first-born spiritual son. Therefore he did not hesitate to beg this special blessing—he had long since learned that Elijah's power had been nothing less than the power of the living Lord present in his spirit. And this he wanted in rich measure.

The powerful prophet reached out his hand and laid it on the younger man's shoulder in a gesture of fatherly affection. Looking straight into his eyes he replied with flaming intensity:

"Elisha—you have asked for a great and good thing. If you see me taken from you it will be so. If not, you will be the loser."

More than ever Elisha's will was set and steeled to stay close to Elijah. He was so glad he had not stayed behind at Gilgal, Bethel or Jericho, or even on the other side of the Jordan. His perseverance would pay off. His loyalty would be vindicated. His faithful fidelity would be honored.

More slowly now the two men trudged on up the hot slopes still warm from the day's desert heat. The last rays of the setting sun turned the gaunt hills of Gilead to gold. Elijah pointed out places where he had roamed as a lad. He showed Elisha where the call of God had come to him fourteen years before to go and challenge Ahab. It was out of these desperate dongas that the flaming firebrand had burst upon the stage of Israel's horrendous history.

Suddenly horses of fire, furiously drawing a chariot of fire, swept out of the evening sky. They rushed past them, drawing Elijah away into the vortex of a powerful whirlwind that followed in its wake. In an instant he was borne away, lost to sight, carried into the celestial realm of a divine dimension.

"My father, my father!" Elisha exclaimed. *"The chariot of Israel and the flaming steeds of God's horsemen."*

It was the end of an era.

It was the flaming farewell for the prophet of power.

It was the appropriate climax to a career in which Elijah's life had burned fiercely with an undiminished incandescence. That inner flame had been nothing less than the presence, power and passion of God's own Spirit.

The same Spirit had now in visible manifestation swept Elijah up in the whirlwind. It was the same honor that previously had been bestowed upon Enoch, who walked with God for 300 years. He, too, bypassed death and was not, for God took him to himself.

During his meteoric career, Elijah had been the voice of God speaking to a decadent nation sunk in debauchery. He had become the conscience of his generation whereby they could still see and know what it was to serve the living God. He had been the living embodiment of faith in action demonstrating the invisible power of God in the face of the most formidable antagonism. He had shown to a skeptical, cynical society that one man with God can be a majority. He had, in a very real sense, been the powerful bastion of godly manhood who like the chariots and horsemen of heaven defended Israel from total destruction. He had become a father to his people and in particular to the young prophet who now bent down to pick up his mantle from the dust, after tearing his own in two.

Elisha's life would prove that Elijah's faith in God was good to the very end. There fell upon the younger prophet the same Spirit, the same power, the same presence of the Living God that had been Elijah's portion.

Elijah had blazed across the desert wastes of a desperate era in human history. He left upon its pages a remarkable record seldom matched by any other man. Uniquely, wondrously, he had been *the prophet of power, God's power*.

Garbed in the worn, stained and dusty mantle of Elijah, Elisha walked back down to the banks of the Jordan. The curious audience of fifty young men peered across the river in the gathering gloom. Elisha stood alone, looking somewhat forlorn, a solitary figure on the far bank.

Yet he was not alone. For there was present with him the Living Spirit of the Living God. In the power and authority of that Spirit which had descended upon him, he, too, took the master's mantle and struck the water.

The current ceased to flow, as it had for Elijah. In calm confidence and quiet certitude Elisha crossed the Jordan to be greeted with awe by his waiting audience. In wonderment they bowed before him. Assuredly they knew that the very same Spirit of God now resided with the younger man.

One question remained to tantalize them. Where had Elijah been taken? Perhaps, like Moses of old, God had chosen to bury his body upon some obscure rugged peak in the eastern wilderness. Despite Elisha's protests to the contrary, the fifty young prophets set out to search all the wild broken country east of Jordan.

It was a pointless performance. No trace of the powerful prophet was ever uncovered. Only the final set of footprints, that he left in the dust, which suddenly terminated next to Elisha's, remained as a reminder of this mighty man of God. Though they returned empty-handed, fully satisfied at last that Elijah had been swept away to a greater glory, the impact of the prophet's life never dimmed in Israel. To this day he is still revered as the prophet of power!